Scuba Equipment Care and Maintenance

by
Michael B. Farley
and
Charles Royer

First Printing, August 1980
Second Printing, May 1981
Third Printing, April 1983

ISBN 0-932248-01-2
Library of Congress Catalog Card Number 80-80731

Copy editing by Lauren Farley
Photos and illustrations by Michael Farley
Cover design and illustration by James Graca

Marcor Publishing, 2685 Bolker Way, Port Hueneme, CA 93041

Table of Contents

Acknowledgements

The authors wish to express their appreciation to the following people for helpful comments and suggestions in reviewing critical portions of the manuscript and in providing information for revisions: Harry and Paula Ruscigno of SEATEC, Orange, California; Fred and Ray Teurman of KING NEPTUNE, Bell Gardens, California; Bob Cranston of DIVING UNLIMITED INTERNATIONAL, San Diego, California; Homer Fletcher (NAUI INSTRUCTOR); Al Thompson of PROFESSIONAL SCUBA RE-PAIR, North Hollywood, California; and Dana Stewart, of PADI INTER-NATIONAL COLLEGE, San Diego, California.

About the Authors

MICHAEL FARLEY . . . . is a NAUI certified diver of 15 years. He is a graduate of the Northrop Institute of Technology, with a specialized degree in aircraft maintenance engineering. He has performed diving-related work for the U.S. Navy, and has field tested diving equipment for manufacturers. Michael Farley is also co-author of the book, DIVING MEXICO'S BAJA CALIFORNIA, a comprehensive diving guide to the Sea of Cortez. He has presented lectures and multi-media shows for national diving conferences, and also serves as a marine naturalist and diving consultant for underwater films and documentaries.

CHARLES ROYER . . . . is a veteran California diver of 18 years, with current certification from NAUI, PADI, YMCA, LA COUNTY and NASDS. He has worked extensively in the sportdiving industry, specializing in retail store management and equipment repair. Charles Royer has previously owned and operating his own scuba equipment repair facility. His professional expertise encompasses all aspects of scuba equipment care and repair. He currently owns and operates a retail dive store facility.

Foreword

SCUBA EQUIPMENT CARE AND MAINTENANCE has been carefully compiled and edited for the purpose of increasing EVERY DIVER'S knowledge of the equipment that he uses and depends upon to practice his sport safely and comfortably. It is designed to guide EVERY DIVER through basic scuba equipment maintenance procedures, as well as provide information on essential aspects of scuba diving equipment design and function.

While there is often more than one "right" or "acceptable" way of doing something, the authors have adhered to procedures and methods that are widely accepted as general standards in the diving industry. They have also drawn upon their own personal and professional diving, travel, photography and equipment repair experience. However, the authors cannot assume liability for the individual interpretation or the practical application of any of the information contained in the text.

Scuba diving is an inherently dangerous sport, and essential repairs on basic life support systems should only be performed by trained technicians. This book is not designed to replace the skills and knowledge of qualified scuba equipment repair specialists. Nor is any of the information contained in this book designed for use by individuals not properly certified and instructed in the use of scuba diving equipment from a qualified instructor or national certifying agency.

SCUBA EQUIPMENT CARE AND MAINTENANCE is designed to enable EVERY DIVER to become as self-reliant, knowledgeable and capable with his equipment as he is with his sport. This book can help EVERY DIVER enhance the life and comfort of his diving equipment, and will reveal ways to save time, money and aggravation. The authors have compiled this informative handbook in the hopes that it may contribute to years of safe and enjoyable sportdiving experiences for EVERY DIVER, from beginning students to the most advanced.

The authors, June 1980.

Michael B. Farley
Charles Royer

Introduction

YOUR DIVING EQUIPMENT

Every diver's equipment needs are unique. The equipment you choose should reflect careful thought and selection. If you are purchasing new gear, consult with your local dive shop to obtain professional equipment counseling. Before making a major purchase, try the equipment out if possible, in order to decide if it will be right for your needs. If you are contemplating the purchase of used gear, exercise caution and check out the condition of both exterior and interior components before making a decision. Also, investigate the availability of parts for any repairs or overhauls that may be needed in the future.

If you are considering upgrading your old gear, don't be afraid to try something new on the market. Diving products being manufactured today are the result of extensive testing and research designed to provide greater safety, comfort and individual choice for the sportdiver. If the equipment is brand new, reflecting a radical design, find out if it will weather market tests before deciding upon the purchase, or ask around for professional opinions and reactions.

YOUR DIVING DOLLARS$$

Once you've invested in a good set of diving gear designed to meet your special diving needs, the next major consideration will be how to protect that investment. Whether you own just a mask, snorkel and fins, or a complete set of scuba gear, every diving dollar that you invest can be maximized through proper equipment maintenance procedures. Scuba equipment can last the diver a very long time when properly maintained, even when subjected to rigorous use.

This book has been compiled with the high cost of diving equipment in mind. It is designed to provide information on how to properly care for your diving equipment once it has been purchased. Proper maintenance procedures can enhance the useful life of your diving equipment, thereby maximizing your diving dollars.

YOUR DIVING SAFETY

The subject of scuba equipment maintenance is a vitally important one in the field of diving education. Using scuba equipment that has been neglected or improperly maintained may be increasing the risk of diving accidents. By learning how to care for all types of diving equipment and their components, from the simplest O-ring to something as complex as your regulator, you can insure not only the safe operation of your equipment but your personal diving safety as well. This book will contribute to the making of safer, more informed and more conscientious divers.

YOUR DIVING FUN

Scuba divers fall into a unique group of out-door sport enthusiasts, whose enjoyment of their sport is highly dependent upon the proper functioning of their equipment. The technical aspects of maintaining, storing, transporting and handling scuba equipment should be a working part of every diver's fundamental knowledge of his sport.

Each year numerous diving excursions are upset by last minute equipment malfunctions, by a lack of spare parts for field repairs, or simply by a lack of basic knowledge concerning the operation of scuba equipment. Don't let equipment trouble ruin your expensive diving vacation. Whether you dive once a week, once a month, or just once a year, you can use this book to increase your chances of trouble-free diving.

EQUIPMENT MANUFACTURERS

Each year a sophisticated array of new diving equipment makes its way from the manufacturers' drawing boards and production lines to the diving market. The latest issue of any diving magazine will attest to the proliferation of diving equipment innovations that characterizes the diving industry today. Never before in the history of sportdiving has there been such a wide variety of equipment available for the individual diver.

This book is not designed to deal individually with every brand and model of diving equipment currently manufactured. It is the consumer's responsibility to obtain and adhere to any instructions, recommendations or specifications issued by the manufacturer for the particular types of diving equipment that he owns. The information contained herein pertains to basic equipment types and shall in no way replace, supercede or contradict the manufacturer's instructions concerning specific designs, brands or models of scuba diving equipment.

PROFESSIONAL DIVE SHOPS

Professional dive shops not only conduct the ordinary business of retail sales, but also provide the sportdiver with a unique line of services and benefits. Dive shops play a key role in the subject of equipment selection, equipment repair and maintenance, and equipment safety and education. They usually carry a substantial stock of spare parts, and are often set up to perform a variety of in-shop repairs. Dive shops can keep you diving safely and comfortably all year round through their visual tank inspection programs and equipment overhaul services.

As an information center, dive shops are a vital link between you, the consumer, and the manufacturers and national agencies. Dive shops provide information on the latest equipment developments, on up-dates for old products, on factory recalls and news from manufacturers, certifying agencies and national publications. Take advantage of contact with your local dive shop to enhance all facets of your sportdiving activities, including your personal equipment maintenance program.

EQUIPMENT RECALLS

Diving equipment manufacturers may occasionally recall from the market equipment that has been found to contain a defect or that is in need of an update in order to make it safer. In the interest of your own safety, it is a good idea to check periodically with your local dive shop for information pertaining to recalls, or to watch for recall notices in trade publications. If in doubt about the integrity of any of your scuba equipment, particularly if it has been purchased second hand, inquire at your local dive shop for information or contact the manufacturer directly. Equipment manufacturer addresses can be obtained through your local dive shop. Remember, equipment recalls can affect new equipment as well as older equipment, so always keep yourself informed of the latest developments concerning the safety of any equipment that you own.

Mask, Snorkel And Fins

With their simple design and construction, your mask, snorkel and fins may seem like virtually indestructible pieces of diving gear. However, it is surprisingly easy to allow them to deteriorate into useless items. Often, while other equipment is painstakingly cleaned and put away, a pile of masks, snorkels and fins is invariably left strewn about to fend for themselves in the hot sun and salt air. They may be the most inexpensive part of your diving gear, but they are indispensable.

CONSTRUCTION

Neoprene — With proper care, black neoprene rubber can hold up under many years of use. However, sooner or later, neoprene will eventually deteriorate, causing a breakdown in the rubber. This is often evidenced by a sticky or gummy appearance of the rubber. With face masks, a prominent indication of this will be a black ring around the diver's face, caused by the deteriorating rubber around the seal. The neoprene rubber compounds used in diving equipment will often vary as to their softness or flexibility from one model to another.

There are three main enemies of neoprene rubber. These are: 1) prolonged exposure to sunlight 2) exposure to chlorine 3) exposure to ozone. In addition, some suntan lotions contain ingredients that will deteriorate rubber rapidly. Paint and gas fumes can also affect rubber products. By minimizing exposure to any of these elements, the life expectancy of the neoprene can be greatly enhanced.

Silicone — Two types of silicone rubber are used in the manufacturing of masks and snorkels. They are: 1) clear silicone, which resembles an opaque see-through plastic material, and 2) black silicone, which is produced by adding carbon to the clear silicone to obtain a black color.

Silicone masks and snorkels are usually more expensive than their neoprene counterparts, due to the higher cost of the material used. However, their added advantages are contributing to their growing popularity among sportdivers. Silicone masks are more comfortable for people with sensitive skin, since nothing in the silicone material has been found to cause the types of allergic skin reactions that are often caused by the carbon or petroleum chemicals in neoprene rubber.

Silicone rubber is impervious to ozone and ultraviolet rays and will not deteriorate like neoprene does. It is also often more appealing in underwater diver photographs, since the translucent quality of the rubber allows extra illumination of the model's face. It is best to use only silicone snorkel keepers with masks and snorkels both made of silicone, however, as use of black rubber snorkel keepers will cause an unsightly discoloration in the silicone.

In terms of its durability and added advantages, silicone rubber is superior to neoprene and will last longer if properly cared for. However, with good care, any diving mask can last the diver a very long time.

Lightweight Plastics — A recent innovation in the construction of diving fins is the use of translucent, lightweight plastics and other fiberglass reinforced materials. This produces a fin that is lighter and more resilient than those made of neoprene, and one that is more attractive in underwater photographs. Most of these new materials are impervious to ozone and ultraviolet rays and are much more durable than neoprene.

CONDITIONING NEW EQUIPMENT

After purchasing a mask, snorkel or set of fins, remove the manufacturer's shipping preservative from the equipment before using it. Many rubber products are coated with ozone and ultraviolet inhibitors by the manufacturer, which will often appear as a white waxy substance on the rubber. This preservative may be easily removed with a mild abrasive such as a toothpaste or ordinary kitchen cleanser. Scrub the lens of the mask thoroughly, inside and out. If this is not done when the mask is new, the mask will have a tendency to fog easily during the dive.

Remove the straps from the mask and from the fins in order to scrub them with cleanser until all of the preservative is removed. This will help prevent the straps from slipping from their adjusted position on the equipment. Replace the straps on the equipment, and adjust them to the proper size. Install the snorkel on the mask so that it fits into your mouth easily and comfortably when needed. If the mouthpiece does not fit comfortably, shop around for a more comfortable fit.

When conditioning new masks made of neoprene rubber, it is best to wash the ''skirt'' of the mask which forms the seal around the diver's face with fresh water only. Mask seals conditioned with detergent can produce a reaction on the wearer's skin as a result of excess detergent collecting around the feathered edges of the seal. This may show up in the form of a black ring around the face. Some types of women's cosmetics as well as some types of skin oils can also produce a reaction with the neoprene and detergent. Ordinarily, a black ring from a neoprene mask signifies deteriorating rubber, but in the case of new masks, it will usually signify some type of reaction from an irritant.

MODIFICATIONS

There are a few simple modifications, or adjustments, that you can easily perform yourself to improve or enhance the comfort and performance of your diving gear.

THREADING OF FIN STRAPS

Tab Inside   Tab Outside

Tape the Straps — After determining the proper fit of your mask and fins, make at least one dive with the equipment to insure that the fit is correct. If hood and booties are to be worn, make the necessary allowance for extra thickness of neoprene. Then, to prevent the straps from slipping out of adjustment, as they may do over a period of time with prolonged use, secure the straps into their adjusted position with duct tape or electricians tape.

The straps may be threaded with the loose ends on the outside, as designed by the manufacturer, or some models allow the straps to be reversed and threaded with the excess on the inside. Either way, if they have been securely threaded, the loose ends should not slip out of adjustment once you've wrapped them securely with tape.

To prevent the tape from unraveling, leave about three to four inches of excess tape both at the beginning and at the end of the wrapping procedure. Wrap the tape snugly, using a liberal amount, then secure the tape by tying together the excess tape that you have left free on both ends in a good square knot. Cut off any excess tape.

Add a Piece of Neoprene — If you want to be able to wear your fins comfortably with or without booties, try adding a piece of neoprene material to the inside of your fin strap where it rubs against the heel of your foot. Cut a scrap of neoprene material to fit the inside back portion of your fin strap. Wrap the neoprene securely with duct tape or electricians tape.

Add a Nylon Line — For extra ease in getting in and out of fins, especially with cold, wet hands or while wearing bulky gloves, attach a three to four-inch length of nylon line to the heel strap, with a small loop or knot in the end for secure grasping. This line should not be long enough to enable it to catch on coral or kelp, and may not be suitable for all diving environments. If it's time to replace your worn-out strap, you can purchase a new fin strap with a pull tab already installed by the manufacturer.

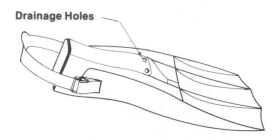

Drainage Holes

Install Drain Holes — In order to aid in draining out sand and water that may become trapped in the foot pocket of your fin, a couple of drain holes may be installed in the toe ends of the foot pockets. If you do a lot of beach diving, this is a must. Some fins already incorporate this feature in their design.

Carefully drill a series of two to three small holes, preferably no larger than 1/4'' each, in either the top or sole of the foot pocket near the toes. If the holes are cut too large, it will negate their function by allowing sand and large particles to seep into the fin through the drainage holes.

You can also install drain holes in your fins by using a length of wire coat hanger or a sturdy nail. Heat the metal over a fire until it becomes red hot. Then, using a pair of pliers for grasping the hot metal, puncture the rubber with the hot coat hanger or nail to create the desired drain holes. The excess rubber around the edges of the holes may be trimmed off with a razor blade.

REPAIRS

Any straps or parts that show signs of excessive wear should be replaced prior to the next dive. If your equipment has been in storage for a period of time, it is extremely important to check the condition of your equipment before diving with it. Even if you do most of your diving close to home, always take an extra fin strap or two and an extra snorkel keeper in your gear bag.

Replacing Broken Mask Lenses — If the lens in your mask becomes cracked or shattered, you usually won't have to throw away the entire mask. Replacement lenses can be purchased or ordered through a dive shop. Some of the newer masks with narrow bridges of glass over the nose and wrap around type masks require precision adjustments to obtain a good seal, so it is best to return the mask to the manufacturer to have the new lens installed.

Damaged or Torn Rubber — If the rubber on your mask or fins becomes torn or damaged, the entire piece of equipment will usually have to be replaced. If you use a full foot fin, be particularly careful not to tear or damage the rubber around the heel as you step in or out of it.

When installing buckles on masks or fins, be careful not to bend or distort the frame of the buckle. If the frame does become distorted, the slide bar will not bind effec-tively, causing the strap to slip out of adjustment.

Installing Buckles — If the attachment buckle on your mask or fins becomes damaged, you can purchase a replacement from your dive shop. It is usually a simple procedure to install the new buckle, unless the buckle has an extra-strength type retaining pin or rivet that requires special tools.

To remove the old buckle, spread the buckle carefully, using two pairs of pliers, each one gripping an opposite end. Separate the buckle apart for-cibly with the pliers, then remove it from the rubber seat, taking care not to damage the rubber. Never pull the buckle out of the rubber, as damage to the rubber may result.

When installing the new buckle, do not distort the buckle when positioning it. Any distortion could impede the movement of the binding slide bar, causing the fin or mask strap to pull loose easily. To install, hook one end of the buckle into the retaining hole in the rubber seat, then lift up and forward to the other end.

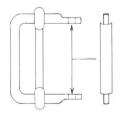

PIN TYPE BUCKLE   **SPLIT BUCKLE**

Replacing a damaged or deteriorated purge valve on a mask is a simple operation, requiring a minimum of parts. Purge valve replacement assemblies for individual masks are available at professional dive shops.

To remove a buckle with a retaining pin, simply hold one end of the buckle with a pair of pliers while lifting the other end of the buckle up and away from the pin, taking care not to lift the buckle far enough to distort it.

To install this type of buckle, first insert the pin into the mask or fin. Next, install one end of the buckle onto the pin. Then gently lift the other end of the buckle with a pair of pliers being careful not to distort it, and install it on the other end of the pin. Check to insure that the binding slide bar travels freely. To insure that the buckle stays securely attached to the pin, the ends of the pin may be lightly center punched, taking care not to distort the pin.

Faulty Purge Valves — If you detect a leaky purge valve on your snorkel or mask, either the neoprene valve or the entire assembly may be replaced or ordered through your local dive shop. Make sure you obtain the proper size for your particular mask or snorkel. If the rubber around the purge valve has deteriorated or torn, this could be the cause of the leakage, necessitating replacement of the entire mask. Always check out this possibility before replacing the purge valve.

The installation of the purge valve assembly is an easy operation. Simply pop out the damaged one, and pop in the new purge valve, taking care not to damage the soft rubber in the mask. For extra security, before installing the purge valve clean the hole in the mask and apply a thin layer of wetsuit cement. Let set until tacky, then install the new purge valve.

PREVENTATIVE MAINTENANCE

Clean-up — After each use, rinse thoroughly in fresh water. Warm water is preferable to cold water for dissolving any encrusted salt particles that may accumulate on the lens of the mask in the narrow recesses around the lens retaining ring. Occasionally wash in warm, soapy water, followed by a thorough rinsing to remove traces of chlorine, perspiration, salt or lotions that may collect on the rubber over a period of time through normal use.

Allow the equipment to dry thoroughly before storage, but do not expose it to sunlight or heat for an extended period of time. For prolonged periods of storage, remove the straps from masks and fins to relieve the stress on the rubber. The rubber may be coated with silicone lubricant to prevent drying and cracking, but avoid spraying the lens of the mask with silicone or grease, as this will prevent it from defogging properly when diving. Surgical grade silicone masks should not be stored or carried in the same bag as other black neoprene products, as they may change color when exposed to black rubber.

Inspection — Periodically check your equipment to inspect for worn parts, replacing where necessary.

1. *Mask Lens* — Inspect for nicks and cracks or chips in the lens of the mask. Never dive with a chipped or cracked lens.

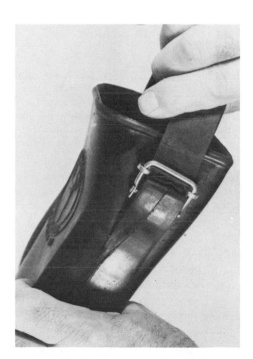

Exposure to such harmful elements as ozone, chlorine, sunlight and salt will cause rubber products to deteriorate rapidly. They should be inspected frequently for signs of cracking and brittleness, indicating that they may need to be replaced.

2. *Lens Retaining Ring* — Inspect for any defects, such as cracks, broken spot welds, stripped screws, or loose nuts, that will affect the security of the retaining ring.

3. *Purge Valve* — If your mask has a purge valve, check it for any signs of leakage or deterioration. Make sure the valve operates freely. With the mask held securely to your face, you should be able to force air out the purge valve by exhaling. Then, inhale to check that the purge valve seals properly. No air should enter the mask through the purge valve.

4. *Straps* — Check the mask and fin straps for any signs of deterioration or distortion of the rubber. Flex the rubber gently when dry and look for signs of cracking and brittleness. This will be most noticeable where the straps bend around the buckles.

5. *Snorkel* — Check for any looseness or separation around the mouthpiece, and check to insure that the mouthpiece has not been bitten through. Inspect the snorkel keeper by giving it a gentle pull to see if the rubber is rotting or cracking.

6. *Attachment Buckles* — Check the mask and fin strap attachment buckles for any signs of spreading or distortion to insure that normal tension will not pull them loose from the rubber.

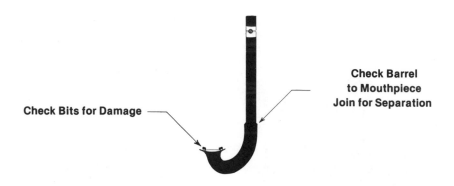

Check Barrel
to Mouthpiece
Join for Separation

Check Bits for Damage

7. *Fins* — If your fins are constructed of a combination of neoprene and plastic, don't forget to check for signs of deterioration in the neoprene foot pocket. While the newer plastic materials used in the fin blade may be impervious to deterioration, the neoprene foot pocket will deteriorate if not properly protected from harmful elements, such as chlorine, ozone or ultraviolet rays.

Wetsuits

Today, wetsuits are being manufactured for the sportdiver in every conceivable style, shape and color combination designed to meet a wide variety of individual diving needs and preferences. Divers all over the world don wetsuits (or drysuits) of varying lengths and thicknesses to protect themselves from such local hazards as chilly water temperatures, stinging marine creatures, abrasions from rocks and coral, and from the burning rays of the tropical sun.

Modern wetsuits are sportier, more colorful and reflect a wider diversification of designs and styles than their basic black rubber ancestors of yesteryear. Beyond purely protective purposes, today's divers choose wetsuits of unique color combinations and custom designs to reflect greater individuality, thus making their wetsuits easier to identify, more attractive to photograph and more comfortable to wear.

WETSUIT CONSTRUCTION

Materials — There are basically two types of neoprene rubber used in the construction of diving suits today. The first type developed and still used is called "chemical blown" neoprene. This consists of mixing a chemical into the neoprene during the curing process to give the rubber a cellular structure. Due to a variety of blending techniques and temperature variations, "chem-blown" neoprene often results in a neoprene material of irregular density and produces a generally stiffer type of rubber.

The second and more recently developed variety is known as "nitrogen-blown" neoprene. This is produced by inducing nitrogen gas into the neoprene to provide a more uniform cellular structure while it is curing. This type of process usually results in a neoprene material of a more regular density, lending greater flexibility and added thermal qualities to the wetsuit.

Nylon is also used in conjunction with neoprene to produce various configurations of nylon and neoprene suits, with the nylon tightly bonded to one or both sides of the neoprene. Since it is primarily the thickness and cellular structure of the neoprene as well as the fit of the suit that determines the warmth of the suit, nylon does not appreciably contribute to the thermal quality of the suit. Rather, the nylon material endows the wetsuit with other added advantages and comforts.

1. *Nylon Inside* — A layer of nylon on the inside of a neoprene wetsuit produces less friction against the body than the rubber, making the suit easier to slip on and off. Wetsuits with nylon on just the inside will usually have textured patterns on the outside neoprene surface, to enhance the fit and flexibility of the suit.

2. *Nylon Outside* — A layer of nylon material bonded to the outside of the suit provides the neoprene with greater resistance to nicks and tears from sharp rocks, coral, barnacles, belt buckles and other sharp objects. It also allows the wetsuit to be made with a variety of colors and patterns. The only disadvantage of a nylon outside cover may be that it retains more moisture than the rubber surface, causing the suit to dry more slowly.

Wetsuits constructed with a nylon covering on just one side of the suit (either inside or outside) are commonly referred to as "Nylon-one" suits, or wetsuits with nylon on just one side. Wetsuits with nylon surfaces on both the inside and outside are referred to as "Nylon-two" suits.

Thickness — Wetsuits of thicknesses varying from 3/16" to 3/8" to as thick as 1/2" are used for diving in cooler water temperatures. If the wetsuit fits poorly, however, it will deter the thickness of the wetsuit from providing the corresponding insulating properties to the body.

For water of mid-temperatures and tropical water, suits of 3/16" and less are used. Thinner suits are not used solely for purposes of warmth, although they do provide a degree of insulation, particularly when diving at depths. Warm water wetsuits are primarily used for protecting the bare skin of a diver from abrasions, stings and other hazards in the marine environment. Snorkelers often wear protective wetsuits to prevent severe sunburns while swimming for prolonged periods with their body exposed to the sun.

Seams — Modern construction techniques allow for the fabrication of wetsuits that are designed to hold up under years of rigorous use by divers, provided they are properly maintained. Once the design of the suit is cut from the neoprene and nylon, manufacturers may combine a variety of glueing and sewing techniques to insure strong, and in many cases, watertight seams.

1. *Glued Seams* — Glued seams are the building blocks of wetsuit construction. Because the glueing of seams is a relatively simple procedure, divers can easily repair seams themselves with the use of commercial neoprene cement sold through professional dive shops. Glued seams are always butt seams, never overlapping, due to the bulkiness of the material.

2. *Sewn Seams* — It was not until the introduction of nylon material into wetsuit construction that stitching could be used to join and reinforce seams effectively. Nylon thread was used in earlier suits, but today, because of its durability and resistance to rotting, Dacron thread is used almost exclusively in wetsuits with sewn seams. Stiching is used to reinforce glued seams, adding greater strength to the existing seam to create a better quality wetsuit.

3. *Taped Seams* — Strips of material running along the inside or outside seams, or along both, indicate an additional method of reinforcing wetsuit seams. A thin strip of neoprene or nylon "tape" may be either glued, sewn or sealed with heat on top of the original seam of the suit to add resistance to tearing and separating.

By examining your own wetsuit, you can easily discover which method of seam reinforcement your manufacturer has used. If a seam begins to tear or separate, always repair it as soon as possible. You can also add strength to existing seams by adding a piece of neoprene or nylon tape over the seam to give it additional reinforcement, if the manufacturer has not already done so.

WETSUIT FASTENERS

Three of the most commonly used fastening devices on wetsuits include the use of zippers, twist-lock assemblies and velcro tabs.

Zippers — Zippers provide the diver with added ease in getting in and out of the wetsuit. For cold water diving, the less zippers a suit has installed in it, the more maintenance free and warmer the suit will tend to be. For beach diving, a minimum of zippers in a suit is also most advantageous, as sand has a tendency to collect in the zippers and can foul or wear the teeth down with prolonged use.

Zippers on wetsuits may be made of plastic, nylon or metal. Aluminum and plated brass are the most common types of metal used. Aluminum is the least expensive, but corrodes easily in salt water. Plated brass zippers are more durable than aluminum since they resist corrosion and are least affected by sand particles. Plastic or nylon zippers are more quickly worn down through hard use around sand than are sturdier, metal zippers.

To lubricate zippers for easier sliding, beeswax, silicone, or even candle wax or soap may be used. Be sure and work the zipper up and down while lubricating. It is a good idea to lubricate all of the zippers before putting the wetsuit away for storage, to insure that they will operate freely the next time you wear it. For beach diving, it is better to use silicone spray, as this will deter large amounts of sand or other particles from adhering to the lubricant on the zipper.

To clean metal zippers anytime corrosion is detected, use a small aluminum wire brush or an ordinary toothbrush. Dip it into a small amount of vinegar, and scrub the zipper until the corrosion is removed. Follow this with a fresh water rinse. Anytime a zipper begins to separate from the wetsuit, repair it immediately. A few strong stitches with Dacron thread should do the job.

Twist-Locks — Some wetsuits have "twist-lock" mechanisms that hook the beavertail flap of a wetsuit jacket or top. These should always be rinsed carefully after diving to remove sand and encrusted salt particles. Twist the fasteners back and forth as they are rinsed. Twist-locks can be bent, or even crushed, quite easily by carelessly tossing a weight belt or tank on them. If this happens, and they can not be straightened out with a pair of pliers to function properly, both grommets and twist-locks can be purchased at a dive shop and easily installed to replace the damaged ones.

The cost for a replacement kit for a twist-lock assembly is minimal. If just the male end has been damaged, due to corrosion or damage from crushing or bending, install a replacement in the following manner.

MALE TWIST-LOCK ASSEMBLY

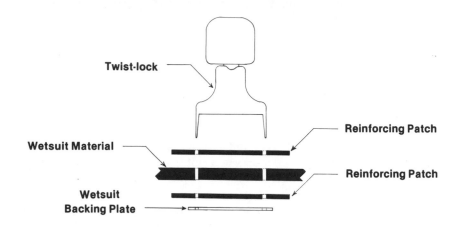

1. Remove the old twist-lock from the suit, by straightening the prongs on the back side of the twist-lock that overlaps a flat washer. Pull the twist-lock out. (NOTE: One type of twist-lock is installed with a hollow rivet instead of with prongs. To remove this type, hold the male end of the fastener securely while cutting off the riveted end of the twist-lock fastener by inserting end cutters between the backing plate of the fastener and the neoprene. Do not cut through the neoprene. Just cut off the end of the rivet and remove the twist-lock fastener from the suit, and install a new fastener in its place.)

2. If the reinforcing pads have also been damaged, new ones of identical size should be installed with wetsuit cement before the new twist-lock is installed in place. Or, if the twist-lock assembly lacks reinforcing pads on either side, this may be a good time to install some yourself for extra strength.

3. Install the new twist-lock through the reinforcing pads and the neoprene. After installing the backing plate, clamp the prongs tightly to assure that it will not pull out. To install the female part of a twist-lock fastener, install in the same manner as the male part, but do not cut the hole in the center until after the fastener has been completely installed.

4. Another type of twist-lock that can be purchased to replace a damaged one consists of a twist-lock assembly already installed on a reinforcing neoprene pad. This type is easily installed by simply glueing the fastener in place using neoprene cement.

REPLACING TWIST-LOCK ASSEMBLIES

1. Remove the old twist-lock from the wetsuit, taking care not to tear the neoprene.

2. Install the new twist-lock assembly in the proper location, replacing the reinforcing pads if necessary.

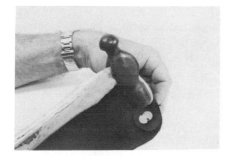

3. Clamp the prongs on the back of the twist-lock tightly over the neoprene to insure sufficient holding strength.

Velcro — Strips of velcro material are being widely used in wetsuit construction to replace zippers and other types of fasteners. Some wetsuits have velcro fasteners around wrist openings, ankles, shoulders, or neck closures to gather the neoprene material tightly to the diver's body. Sand or other foreign particles can accumulate in the velcro strips, seriously affecting the holding strength of the material. If this happens, simply clean the material with a stiff nylon brush, such as a toothbrush, until all traces are removed. If the velcro becomes worn out, it can be replaced by installing an identical strip in its place.

To install velcro so it will function to its maximum capacity of strength, it should be sewn to the suit. If the wetsuit does not have a nylon exterior or interior, to which the velcro can be sewn, then some type of nylon backing material may be used. Dacron thread should be used, and an industrial-type sewing machine may have to be used, depending upon the thickness of the neoprene.

WETSUIT ACCESSORIES

Booties — Booties are usually made with 1/4" or 3/16" neoprene. Soft sole booties are made of the same material throughout, and do not provide any type of reinforcement for the sole. They should not be used out of the water for walking on rocks or other rough surfaces. Hard sole booties have an extra layer of harder textured rubber material on the sole. They are usually more expensive than the soft sole type, but will hold up better under rugged wear and will last longer.

Most of the damage to booties is done while taking them on or off, when trying to force them over the heel of the foot and ripping them in the process. It is very easy to pull out the seam in the back of the bootie or at the point where the sole is joined to the booties (on hard sole booties). A thin pair of nylon socks worn under the booties will help alleviate the possibility of ripping your bootie, by making the bootie slide easily over the heel and entire foot. A thin pair of socks can also prevent chafing around the ankles or toes that may be caused by bulky inner seams, particularly when diving for prolonged periods of time.

Tears or nicks in booties should be repaired as soon as they are detected. If the backseam starts to separate, it can be glued together and reinforced with a strip of neoprene tape glued directly over the seam on the outside of the bootie. However, if the sole on a hard sole bootie is ripped apart from the bootie, this is a difficult spot to repair, and often the entire bootie must be replaced.

For extra aid in drainage when leaving the water, a small hole may be pierced in the toes of a bootie using a large nail. Do not cut a hole and remove any neoprene, however, as this will allow water to enter during the dive and will detract from the thermal quality of the bootie.

Pockets — Utility pockets or pocket-type knife pouches are often added to wetsuits as custom features. While it is possible to install these items yourself if you so desire to modify your wetsuit, it is usually better to contact a qualified wetsuit repair specialist or manufacturer to do the installation for you.

Since pockets protrude from the wetsuit surface, they are particularly susceptible to being snagged or torn on rocks or coral. Glueing alone will usually not provide enough strength for the frequent use that pockets and knife pouches receive. In addition to being glued to the wetsuit, pockets should be sewn securely through the entire thickness of the wetsuit, and further sealed with tape on both the inside and outside for maximum protection from tearing out and damaging the wetsuit.

Knee Pads — Knee pads are often added to wetsuits to reinforce the knees or to patch existing holes in the knees. The knee area frequently receives more wear and tear through constant bending, climbing, crawling, and "walking" on the bottom with your knees. Knee pads may be somewhat restrictive in a new suit (especially if it is a 1/4" or thicker suit), so it is best to let the suit wear a little before adding them.

If it is time to reinforce the knees of your wetsuit, the following procedure may be used to install knee pads:

1. Determine the size of the area to be patched, and cut a corresponding shape (usually rectangular) from a piece of neoprene of at least the next gauge smaller than your wetsuit. The patch should be cut from nylon-one neoprene (nylon on one side). Make sure to cut the patch with a beveled cut, so the edges are beveled inward with the nylon on the outside.

2. Cut the edges of the rectangular (or square) patch to a rounded shape, so that there are no square edges remaining on the patch.

3. Put on the wetsuit, position the patch in the desired place, and draw around the patch while holding it firmly against the wetsuit (you may need help from a buddy to do this). HINT: Avoid positioning the top or bottom edge of the patch too close to the break in the knee, since the constant bending of the knee and stretching of the neoprene in this crucial area will weaken the seam of the patch, and may eventually cause it to tear away from the wetsuit.

4. Use clear neoprene cement when applying to a nylon suit, to avoid unsightly seepage that black cement may cause around the knee pad. Apply as per instructions on the wetsuit cement label.

5. Finish the patch on nylon suits by stitching around the edge of the patch with Dacron thread. It is not necessary to stitch through the entire thickness of the suit, but will suffice to stitch the nylon of the suit to the nylon layer of the patch.

Spine Pads — Spine pads are modifications to wetsuits that provide extra warmth by filling the gap between the spine and the wetsuit jacket or farmer john top. If the hollow space in the natural curve of your back is sufficient to create an air gap between you and your wetsuit, water can flow through this space, creating an uncomfortable and constant flow of cold water.

A spine pad can be installed on a wetsuit by the manufacturer, by a dive shop that offers wetsuit repair services, or by the diver himself. To add a spine pad to your wetsuit, the following procedure may be used:

1. Determine the desired length of the spine pad by measuring the distance between the middle of your shoulder blades and the small of your back.

2. Cut one strip of neoprene approximately two to three inches wide to the desired length. Use a beveled cut, with the edges beveled in toward the rubber side. For this strip, use nylon-one neoprene of the next smaller gauge than your wetsuit.

3. Cut a second strip of neoprene from nylon-one neoprene that is approximately one inch wide and two inches shorter than the first strip (see step #2 above). This strip may be of the same thickness as your wetsuit.

4. Position the narrow strip in the center (both length and width-wise) of the larger strip. Glue the strips together with the rubber sides face-to-face and the nylon on the outsides.

5. With chalk or a pencil, mark the area in the wetsuit where the spine pad will be positioned. On wetsuits with farmer john tops, the spine pad should go inside the farmer john top, where it will give maximum protection to the spine.

6. Install the double-stripped spine pad, rubber side down, to the inside of the wetsuit top or jacket. Use a commercial neoprene cement and apply as per instructions on the container.

7. After the glue has dried thoroughly, the spine pad should be stitched with Dacron thread, catching the nylon material on both the spine pad and the inside of the wetsuit. If the wetsuit and/or spine pad are rubber only, then the beveled edges of the spine pad should be glued securely and pinched tightly against the wetsuit material to form a good sealing edge.

WETSUIT REPAIRS

Wetsuits are susceptible to snags and tears from abrasive surfaces and sharp objects. Small tears and gouges can be easily repaired with a can of wetsuit cement, and larger holes can be repaired with a neoprene patch. Commercial wetsuit cement is sold through most professional dive shops. The instructions on the cans are precise and easy to follow.

To Repair Small Tears — Locate the tear that is to be repaired. Make sure the area around it is clean and dry. Separate the edges of both sides of the tear. Hold them apart by pinching them, or by placing a piece of sturdy cardboard or styrofoam underneath and pinning the edges so they are forced apart.

Coat both sides of the tear with neoprene cement. Let dry until tacky. Then apply another coat of cement, and allow it to dry. The edges must not be allowed to touch each other. After the second coat of cement is dry, press the surfaces back together and pinch them tightly. Pressure should be applied for at least ten minutes. Let the repaired area dry for another six to eight hours before using the suit.

To Patch a Wetsuit — Anytime material is gouged or torn out of a wetsuit, and the material can not be sealed back together with wetsuit cement, it should be patched. To install a patch to your wetsuit, the following steps may be used:

1. Assure that the wetsuit is clean and dry. Determine the size of the area to be repaired. Make a template, or pattern, out of cardboard by cutting a piece that matches the size of the area to be repaired. Usually a circular or rectangular patch with rounded corners is best. Do not use corrugated cardboard to construct the template.

2. Position the cardboard pattern over the damaged area. Draw around the pattern with a pen or pencil that marks the nylon or rubber.

3. Remove the pattern, but don't discard. Place another piece of cardboard behind the area being repaired. This will prevent cutting the material underneath or having the glue soak through.

4. Using sharp scissors, cut out the damaged portion of the wetsuit, following the pattern markings precisely and making clean, straight cuts in the neoprene. Discard the material that has been cut out.

5. Select a piece of material of matching thickness and color of the area being repaired, or choose a contrasting color if you prefer. Using the cardboard pattern, position it over the patching material, drawing around it to get the correct size. Cut evenly and precisely.

6. Without glueing, fit the patch into the hole in the wetsuit to assure a proper fit. If the patch is too large, trim the edges. If the patch is too small, you will have to start over and make a new patch.

7. Remove the patch from the wetsuit. Apply a coat of neoprene cement around its edges, and another coat around the edges of the hole in the wetsuit. Apply a second coat and allow it to dry, following the instructions on the wetsuit cement container.

8. Apply the patch to the wetsuit, assuring proper alignment BEFORE the glued edges are allowed to touch. After the patch is in place, "pinch" around the edges assuring that the neoprene adheres together. Let dry six to

eight hours before using. Nylon material may be further stitched around the edges with Dacron thead.

NOTE: For areas around the knee that are to be patched in this manner, install knee pads over the patch for added reinforcement. Allow the edges of the knee pads to extend out over the edges of the patch at least an inch.

PATCHING A WETSUIT

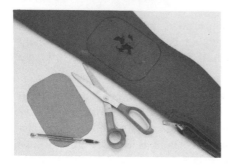

1. Assemble the necessary materials, and mark the area to be patched.

2. Cut out the damaged neoprene and construct a patch using a cardboard template.

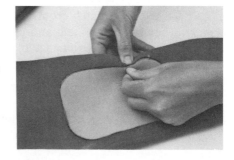

3. Apply two coats of neoprene cement to the edges of the patch and the hole in the wetsuit.

4. Install the patch, pinching the edges tightly to insure that it adheres properly.

WETSUIT ALTERATIONS

If you are a novice at working with neoprene cement, don't attempt to make any alterations to your wetsuit until you have experimented with cutting and glueing procedures using odd scraps of neoprene. As in any tailoring, measurements and cuttings must be exact. Minor alterations, such as taking in slack, lengthening a beavertail, or adding an insert may be done at home, in much the same way as making repairs or installing patches. Leave major alterations for professional repairmen or manufacturers. Be your own judge, and remember, wetsuit material is expensive.

For excess slack in the arms, sides or back, you can easily take out the extra material to obtain a better fit. Make sure it is an area that does not require precision tailoring involving darts or biased seams. Have a buddy help you determine the amount of slack to be taken out. Make a chalk mark on both sides of the slack material. Cut out the overage, making nice clean cuts. Always cut conservatively, in case your measurements have not been exact. Glue the cut edges back together as per instructions on the wetsuit cement label. Allow the seam to dry overnight before using the wetsuit again. The seam may be reinforced, if so desired, with a strip of neoprene or nylon tape, either glued or sewn on top of the altered seam.

Wetsuit cement should always be handled very carefully. Do any repairs or alterations over a piece of cardboard or heavy paper, as glue is difficult to remove from carpets and furniture.

WETSUIT CARE

1. Wash thoroughly after every dive with warm, fresh water. If possible, let it soak in a tub or other large container, giving it several fresh water rinses.

2. To protect the rubber and eliminate any odors, periodically rinse the suit with a commercial wetsuit conditioner or with a mixture of baking soda and water to disinfect and clean the suit.

3. Rinse the suit and allow it to dry. It is best to hang the suit up to allow it to air dry. Use very WIDE hangers, with at least three-inch wide shoulders, to prevent the rubber from creasing or stretching the suit.

4. Check for any leaks or tears while washing the suit, particularly around the seams, knees and the seat. Fill different parts of the wetsuit with water for a balloon effect, and mark any spots where the water leaks out. Repair any leaks with wetsuit cement only after the suit is completely dry.

5. Work the zippers and twist-locks while rinsing, to insure that all salt is rinsed free from tiny crevices. Lubricate the wetsuit zippers with silicone or beeswax to prevent corrosion (for metal zippers) and to insure smooth operation for future dives.

6. Make sure the suit is completely dry before storage. Always store it at a constant temperature, away from smog, heat and sunlight. If you store your wetsuit on a hanger, make sure it is a wide, smooth hanger. Never fold or stuff the wetsuit into a diving bag for storage.

ABOUT DRYSUITS

Drysuits are a unique type of exposure suit, designed for diving in cold water environments. A drysuit is a one-piece inflatable suit constructed of wetsuit material. The air is trapped inside the suit with the aid of watertight seals at the wrist, neck and ankles of the suit, and the trapped air is then used for insulation from the cold water.

An inflator mechanism mounted on the chest of the suit allows the diver to inflate the suit to control the air supply inside.

The wrist, ankle and neck seals are usually fabricated of 1/8" or 3/16" nylon-in/rubber-out neoprene material. It is very pliable rubber and can tear out easily if proper care is not taken while getting in and out of the suit. Never put undue stress on the seal material, and never allow the rubber seals to become dry and brittle.

Drysuits also incorporate a waterproof zipper assembly to prevent the water from entering. The zipper is an important part of the watertight integrity of the suit. It should be cleaned thoroughly after every dive with warm, fresh water, and lubricated periodically with beeswax to preserve its flexibility and to insure that it seals and operates properly. Drysuits should be stored with the zipper assembly left open so as not to put undue stress on the rubber seals.

During normal diving, punctures and tears will occasionally occur. Drysuits should be tested and repaired routinely. The following is an effective method of checking drysuits for leaks:

1. Install small tapered-neck bottles in the wrist and ankle seals (if booties are not attached). Install a large coffee can or something similar in the neck seal. Wrap velcro bands or cotton cord (avoid using tape) around the neck, wrist and ankle seals in order to make the suit airtight. Take care not to damage the neoprene seals. Close the waterproof zipper. Inflate the suit with the oral inflator. Caution: Do not overinflate or you may damage the suit.

2. Mix a strong solution of dish detergent and water, and brush over all seams and the zipper, checking for any leaks which will be evidenced by a bubbling action of the soap caused by escaping air. Then brush over entire suit, checking carefully around the armpit, crotch, knee and elbow areas. Afterward, be sure to rinse the suit thoroughly, removing all traces of detergent.

A new method recently developed by DUI (a drysuit manufacturer in San Diego) to repair minor seam and pinhole material leaks quickly and simply is by injecting urethane into the material to fill the leak. This repair method is available at their factory, or may be available through dive stores.

Tanks
Valves and Backpacks

Until the late 1940's, a hydrostatic test once every five years was effective in detecting normal wear and tear on high pressure gas cylinders. Then, as scuba diving began its steady ascent into popularity, the situation altered. Along with an increase in the number of scuba divers came an increase in the use and handling of high pressure cylinders around corrosion producing elements and potential sources of contamination.

As a result, today in addition to the hydrostatic test, other maintenance procedures are necessary to insure the integrity and continuing use of high pressure cylinders for scuba diving. Compressed air cylinders require special precautions in maintenance, handling and storing to insure maximum tank life and optimum safety for the diver.

ABOUT STEEL TANKS

Exterior Coatings — All steel tanks manufactured for scuba today are galvanized (coated with zinc) to prevent rust from forming on the bare steel. This is the best method of exterior tank protection. A zinc coating exhibits a gray to silvery appearance, characteristic of a majority of steel tanks in use today.

Epoxy or vinyl coatings are used in conjunction with a zinc coating, since they do not last long enough by themselves to provide adequate protection against rust. They protect the zinc from chipping and also add an eye-appealing coat of color or finish to the tank. Some earlier types of tanks were not protected with galvanization, and they generally require more maintenance since they lack the protective undercoating of zinc.

Interior Linings — To protect the interior of the tank from corrosion caused by moisture entering the tank, some manufacturers lined the interior of the tank with either a white coating of paint, a blue plastic coating, or a reddish-brown epoxy coating. When applied properly and evenly, these coatings were effective in preventing water from coming in direct contact with the interior tank walls, thus discouraging the formation of rust. Most of the tanks manufactured between 1954 and 1974 contained some type of interior lining.

Today, however, all manufacturers of scuba cylinders have discontinued the use of interior linings in tanks as a result of maintenance problems generated by the linings. If even the smallest pinhole develops in the lining, moisture can find its way under the lining. Rust will begin to form, eventually working its way under the lining and lifting it loose from the tank as the corrosion spreads. This process is almost unnoticeable to the naked eye.

Also, some linings have a tendency to flake off after just a few years in service. If these tiny particles go undetected, they can travel through the tank valve and into the regulator, causing contamination to both. Don't completely trust a lining to protect the interior of your tank. A lined cylinder should be inspected just as frequently as an unlined cylinder, and the lining should be removed at the first sign of deterioration.

Corrosion — Corrosion in steel tanks involves an oxidation process whereby oxygen in the air combines with the iron, causing a deterioration or "eating away" of the metal. The residue formed by this process is called rust, or iron oxide. Rust is the number one enemy of steel tanks. Steel tanks will rust readily, while aluminum tanks do not rust at all (though they do have their own peculiar brand of corrosion called aluminum oxide).

Normally, the oxidation process in steel occurs very slowly, or does not occur at all if the metal does not come in direct contact with oxygen. However, when the bare metal is exposed to both oxygen and water vapor, the oxidation process accelerates. And exposure to salt water accelerates the process even more. Salt water in steel tanks can ruin the tank in less than three months, rendering it useless for compressed air storage.

ABOUT ALUMINUM TANKS

Construction — Aluminum tanks were first introduced commercially into the United States in the early 1970's, although other types were used in Europe as early as 1930. Since pure aluminum is too weak to withstand high pressures, the aluminum used to manufacture scuba tanks is actually an aluminum alloy, whose additives endow the metal with high strength and corrosion resistant properties. Some aluminum tanks are protected with an anodized coating on the outside, and most are painted externally with a polyurethane enamel.

Corrosion — Aluminum tanks are more resistant to corrosion, due to characteristics inherent in the metal itself. Rust (iron oxide) will not form on aluminum, and aluminum tanks are not susceptible to the corrosive effects of oxidation found on steel tanks. The corrosion that does take place on aluminum tanks produces a thin, powdery substance called *Aluminum Oxide*. This thin residue adheres to the bare metal underneath and actually protects the metal from any further corrosion.

EFFECTS OF CORROSION

Corrosion in steel tanks may range from a light surface coat the consistency of dust, to severe pitting or cratering which can eat its way through the walls of the cylinder very quickly. A light coat of corrosion may be removed by having the tank tumbled by a reputable facility. However, if the damage is too severe, the tank will have to be condemned and can not be used for the storage of pressurized gases.

Besides damaging the tank itself, an accumulation of corrosion in a tank can also cause other problems. Tiny corrosion particles can become lodged in the tank valve or regulator, causing malfunctions to either or both. In severe cases, the amount of oxygen within the tank itself is reduced. A diver using an extremely corroded tank could run the risk of becoming unconscious underwater, since corrosion accumulation in the tank could seriously deplete the oxygen in the air that is being breathed.

Corrosion in aluminum tanks will usually not cause serious deterioration of the tank, since once an adequate coating of aluminum oxide is formed, further corrosion ceases. However, the powdery substance can flake off from the cylinder walls and find its way into the valve or regulator. An aluminum tank should be inspected just as often as a steel tank.

REMOVING CORROSION

Aluminum Tanks — Aluminum oxide will form on the tank exterior anywhere there is a nick, scratch or gouge in the protective coating, and the bare metal is exposed to the elements. A white, chalk-like deposit will form over the damaged area. The corrosion can be removed by using a small piece of aluminum wool or a square of wet/dry sandpaper of a light grit on the affected area. The edges should be feathered for repainting. If the damage is excessive, the entire tank may be repainted, or the damaged areas may be touched up with a like color of enamel.

A light coating of aluminum oxide in the interior may be removed by rinsing the tank with distilled water, then drying the interior thoroughly using an effective warm air flow source. The tank valve should not be replaced until all traces of moisture and foreign particles have been removed and the tank is completely dry inside.

If the tank is severely corroded, a visual inspector will usually recommend that the tank be sent to a hydro testing facility, where an assortment of different cleaning agents will be used, depending upon the severity of the corrosion. Aluminum tanks are soft and should never be subjected to a "heavy tumble" to remove corrosion. Tumbling the tank with hard abrasive materials (such as is done with steel tanks) may remove the inner anodized coating and can damage the bare metal.

Steel Tanks — Corrosion on the exterior of a steel tank may be removed in a variety of ways, depending upon the extent of the corrosion. The most common method of removing rust from the exterior for light surface corrosion is a light sandblasting. This removes all of the rust from the pores of the metal. The entire tank, or just the affected area, should then be recoated with zinc. If further protection is desired, a paint or epoxy can be applied. A zinc coating provides the best protection, as paint and epoxies may chip easily and don't last as long. Never use a grinder on a steel tank and never do any type of welding on a tank.

If the tank is severely corroded on the exterior surface, it should be sent to a hydro testing facility where they can determine the extent of the damage to the structure of the cylinder and recommend further corrective measures.

Interior Rust in steel tanks is usually removed by a process called "tumbling". Different types of abrasives, determined by the magnitude of the corrosion, are used to remove the rust. The tank is filled half full with abrasive materials, then rotated by a special process until all rust is removed from the cylinder walls. If salt water is found inside a tank and it is verified that corrosion hasn't had a chance to start yet, the cylinder may be rinsed with distilled water and dried thoroughly, being careful not to replace the valve until all moisture has been removed. It should be kept in mind, however, that on a clean steel tank, rust can begin to form in as little as three minutes.

CONTAMINATION

In addition to problems caused by rust and aluminum oxide, scuba tanks can also be contaminated from faulty filtration systems in air compressors. One such type of contamination involves carbon particles in the form of activated charcoal that is used for filtration purposes in compressors. Carbon particles can enter the tank during the air fill if they have not been filtered out prior to the air entering the cylinder. Carbon is not harmful to the tank itself, but it can cause malfunctions in the tank valve and regulator. (This problem is never present in air compressors with cartridge type filters.)

Carbon inside a tank can be visually detected by its black and dry appearance. Or, black particles may show up around the inlet hole on the tank valve. Inspect this area after each air fill before connecting your regulator. If allowed to persist in the tank, the particles can lodge themselves in the tank valve, causing the tank valve to seat improperly. These particles may also plug the wafer filter at the entrance to the first stage of the regulator, or may lodge in the first stage high pressure valve or second stage low pressure valve, causing the regulator to malfunction.

KEEPING MOISTURE OUT OF YOUR TANK

The obvious way to prevent corrosion in both aluminum and steel tanks is to prevent water from coming in contact with the tank metal for any length of time. The following recommendations will insure that water will not have a chance to damage your tank.

1. Never drain the air completely out of a scuba cylinder, and never leave the valve open if you do. If you do drain a tank completely dry during a dive, close the tank valve immediately. Then, at the earliest opportunity the valve should be removed to check for water in the interior of the tank.

2. Never let the air escape from the tank rapidly. If you must let the air out of your tank, do it slowly. The best method is to immerse the tank in shallow water with the valve above water, and slowly let the air escape. Emptying the tank in a hurry will cause condensation of moisture to form on the interior of the tank. As the air inside expands rapidly, it will also cool very rapidly, giving up some of its water vapor in the process.

3. Make sure all fittings are dry when attaching a regulator or a filler nozzle from a compressor to the tank valve. One way to insure this is to momentarily open the tank valve and purge it before filling the tank or attaching the regulator. This will blow away any drops of moisture that may have accumulated near the opening. If even a few drops of water enter the tank, they can cause corrosion inside the tank over a period of a few short months.

4. When washing your tank, pay attention to the tank boot and the backpack attachments. Water trapped in tightly fitted areas may enter small nicks and scratches and begin corrosion on the exterior of the tank.

PROPER TANK HANDLING AND MAINTENANCE

In addition to insuring that water is never allowed to enter or form inside your tank, you should take the following precautions in handling and maintaining your scuba tank.

1. Always give your tank a fresh water rinse before putting it away. Be sure the tank valve is *closed* when running water over it.

2. Do not overfill your tank past stamped ratings. This places too much stress on the metal, causing the tank to weaken over a period of time.

3. Avoid rough handling that will cause dents, gouges or nicks in the tank. This can invite corrosion of the metal, and can also weaken the cylinder.

4. Do not store tanks that are full of air for prolonged periods of time. A tank should be stored with just enough air pressure (100 to 200 psi) to keep moisture out. Remember: the higher the tank pressure, the greater the corrosion that may form inside.

5. Always store tanks in a vertical position unless recommended otherwise by a visual inspector. If there is any moisture in the tank, corrosion

may form on the bottom of the tank, which is the thickest part of the tank wall.

6. If you see or smell anything coming out of the tank valve, corrosion or contamination may be suspected. If you rap on the side of the tank and hear anything rattling around inside, the tank should be opened for a visual inspection.

7. If water is found inside the tank, but corrosion has not yet become pronounced, the tank can be rinsed in fresh water or steam cleaned, then dried thoroughly with warm air. It is always best to let a qualified inspector determine the extent of the corrosion.

8. Your tank should receive a *visual inspection* at least once a year. If the tank is in constant use or is constantly filled around salt air, then it should be visually inspected more often, or every three to six months. This is one of the most important and economical preventative maintenance procedures that you can follow to enhance the life of the scuba tank.

9. You must have the tank *hydrostatically* tested at least once every five years. This should only be performed by a reputable hydro testing facility that is able to totally service your tank, including testing, cleaning, drying, zinc coating and painting.

10. If you suspect anything wrong with your scuba cylinder, always have it visually inspected by a professional dive shop or by a reputable repair facility.

WHAT IS A VISUAL INSPECTION?

Visual tank inspections are the diver's best insurance against corrosion and contamination of the scuba cylinder. There is no law that requires visual inspections, but they should be performed as often as necessary for the safety of both the individual diver and of those filling or handling scuba tanks.

The amount of use a scuba cylinder receives is a good indication of how often it should receive a visual inspection. The more you use the tank, the greater chance it has of becoming contaminated or corroded. Every scuba tank should be inspected both externally and internally *at least once a year,* and more frequently if any of the following conditions prevail:

1. Always inspect a tank that has been in storage for an extended period of time before using it.

2. If the tank is subjected to rigorous use, it should be inspected at least once every three to six months.

3. Scuba tanks that are consistently filled around salt air should be inspected every three to six months, depending upon the frequency of their use.

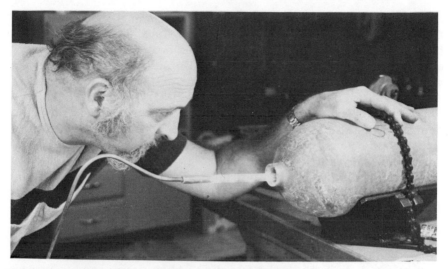

Visual tank inspections are performed by qualified inspectors who can accurately assess the condition of the interior and exterior tank surfaces. A special light is used for critical examination of the interior cylinder walls.

4. Any time the tank is completely drained of air, it should receive a visual inspection.

5. Anytime signs of corrosion or contamination are detected (strange odors, unusual noises in the tank, foreign particles around the valve, etc.) the tank should be given a visual inspection.

6. Anytime a tank valve or regulator malfunctions, the tank should be suspected for possible contamination or corrosion, and if so warranted, should receive a visual inspection.

7. Anytime the tank valve is removed from the cylinder, (for maintenance or other purposes), give the tank a visual inspection before reinstalling the valve.

8. Anytime the integrity of the tank is in question, such as after damage from fire or dents or gouges, it should be given a visual inspection and sent to a testing facility.

9. Whenever purchasing a used scuba cylinder, always have it visually inspected and check to insure that the proper blow plug has been installed.

Use the visual tank inspection program as a tool to obtain maximum service and safety from your scuba cylinder. It will also enhance the life of your tank valve and regulator.

PROCEDURES FOR A VISUAL INSPECTION

Visual inspection procedures are relatively simple and involve a minimum of time and expense. However, to obtain the greatest benefit from the inspection, it should be performed by qualified persons who are familiar with the characteristics and appearance of corrosion and contamination. Anyone can look inside a tank, but only a trained eye can properly evaluate what's going on inside the tank in order to recommend corrective action, if required.

A visual tank inspection may be obtained through your local dive shop or at a reputable hydro testing facility or scuba repair center for a nominal fee. Always obtain a receipt from the tank inspector with the tank serial number and date written in just in case the sticker or decal comes off of the cylinder. A visual inspection will usually involve the following procedures:

1. External conditions of the tank are noted. After removal of the backpack and tank boot, the external surface is inspected for signs of corrosion or obvious signs of damage.

2. The air is then completely drained from the tank, very slowly. The tank is locked into a chain vice in order to hold it secure and to prevent damage to the tank exterior.

3. After assuring that no air is left in the cylinder, the tank valve is removed by using the proper tool so as not to damage the valve.

4. After removing the valve, a light source of sufficient intensity is inserted through the tank neck. The interior of the tank is then visually inspected for any signs of corrosion or contamination. The threads of the tank neck are also inspected for damage.

5. If any problems are found, corrective action will be recommended by the inspector. This may range from an internal rinsing and drying to remove light corrosion, to "tumbling" by a reputable facility to remove heavier corrosion.

6. If the strength of the tank is in question, it will be sent to a hydro testing facility for further treatment and inspection. If the cylinder passes the visual inspection, the valve is reinstalled on the tank, and the tank is refilled with air while checking for leaks around the valve assembly.

7. After the visual inspection, a sticker or stamp decal is then applied to the tank exterior, indicating the month and year of the inspection. This will enable the next person who fills the tank to know when the tank was last inspected.

WHAT IS A HYDRO?

The term "hydro" is short for hydrostatic testing. The hydrostatic or hydro test is one that has been developed by the I.C.C. (*Interestate Commerce Commission)* and is now under the jurisdiction of the D.O.T. *(Department Of Transportation)*. The hydro test measures the strength of the tank walls under special pressurized conditions in order to determine if the scuba tank is still safe enough to be used. The hydro facility will also give the tank a thorough visual inspection, both internal and external.

The hydro test should be performed by a reputable hydro testing facility. (In the U.S., the facility should be authorized by the Bureau of Explosives.) The first part of the test consists of an internal and external visual inspection of the tank. Then the hydro facility will perform the hydrostatic pressure test on the tank. The pressure test is the same for both aluminum and steel tanks. If the tank passes the hydro test, then it will be stamped accordingly with a new date. If the tank fails any part of the testing, the examiner will condemn the tank. Only a reputable hydrostatic testing facility is authorized to condemn a tank.

A hydro test is required by law once every five years, for continuing use of a scuba cylinder. However, anytime the integrity of the tank is in question once it has received a visual inspection, it should be sent to a hydro facility. And, anytime the tank has been subjected to heat damage, it should receive a hydrostatic test.

Heat Damage — Steel tanks that have been damaged by fire or smoke must be tested prior to placing them back into use. Aluminum tanks that have suffered fire or smoke damage are automatically condemned by the testing facility. Aluminum tanks that have been exposed to elevated temperatures should be hydrostatically tested before filling to test for any loss of cylinder strength. Anytime an aluminum tank becomes heated over 180 °F, its heat treatment protection begins to be damaged. (The Compressed Gas Association specifies that an aluminum cylinder which has been exposed to more than 350 °F shall be condemned.)

Paint Processes — Care should always be taken not to expose aluminum tanks to elevated temperatures. Certain painting or refinishing processes involve curing or baking at high temperatures, and these should never be used on aluminum tanks. If you are planning to have your scuba tank repainted, be sure that no heat is applied to the tank in the process. If in doubt about the type of paint process used on an aluminum cylinder, it is best to have the tank hydrostatically tested before filling to test the safety of the cylinder. Compressor operators are wary of freshly painted aluminum cylinders, and may want to verify that a hydro test was completed AFTER the new paint job.

PURCHASING USED TANKS

Scuba tanks change hands frequently. If you are considering buying used scuba equipment, consider the following precautions concerning scuba tanks:

1. Never assume that the tank is in good condition, even if it is shiny and new looking. Always insist that the tank be inspected both externally and internally by a qualified repair facility. Do not complete the purchase if

no new hydro date (within the last 12 months) is stamped on the tank.

2. Try to determine what was previously stored in the tank (other gases besides air), and for how long. Special cleaning procedures may be necessary to remove any traces of potentially harmful gases.

3. Check to see what type of tank valve is used on the neck. Is it an unusual fitting or valve that will be difficult to repair or find replacement parts. Also check to see that the proper burst disc is in the tank valve.

4. Always compare the purchase price with the existing value of new tanks, taking into consideration the cost of corrective measures (hydro test, tumbling, painting) that may be required to restore the tank to safe use. Know what you're buying before taking a "bargain-priced" tank home only to find out later that it won't pass a hydro test.

5. Remember, if you are purchasing a used aluminum tank that has been painted with anything other than the manufacturer's paint, it is recommended that it undergo a hydro test, unless you can verify that it was painted with a process that does not involve temperature exposure.

TANK SYMBOLS — WHAT DO THEY MEAN?

Whether purchasing new or used tanks, you should be aware of what the hyroglyphics on the neck of the tank mean, as they reveal valuable information about the tank. Since scuba tanks have long lives, some of the information given here may not pertain to the older tanks. Both steel and aluminum tanks come in several different sizes.

ALUMINUM TANK

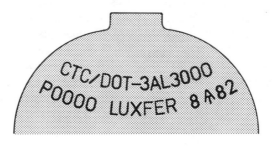

Aluminum Tanks — Luxfer USA currently produces all aluminum tanks made in the U.S. and Canada. The letters, numbers and symbols on the illustrated aluminum tank neck indicate the following information:

CTC — stands for CANADIAN TRANSPORTATION COMMISSION, the equivalent of the U.S. Department of Transportation (DOT). This indicates that the tank meets Canadian regulations and can be sold in that country.

DOT — *Department of Transportation.* The regulation of scuba cylinders falls under their jurisdiction in order to set safety standards for manufacturing, testing and transporting.

3AL — As of July 1, 1982, the DOT adopted new regulations requiring that all aluminum scuba tanks be stamped 3AL, which indicates the DOT specified aluminum alloy of which the tank is made.

(Prior to that date, each manufacturer was assigned a number beginning with an E or SP and that number had to appear on the tanks the company made. The designation E or SP 6498, for example, stamped on tanks manufactured prior to July 1982 would indicate the permit number of the manufacturer. When the older E and SP tanks are next hydro tested, they will also have to be stamped with the DOT specified 3AL.)

3000 — The number (in this case 3000) that comes after the 3AL is the service pressure of the tank. This means that the tank can be filled to 3,000 pounds per square inch (psi) maximum. The tank should never be filled to a higher pressure than the one indicated. Currently, all of the aluminum tanks available have working pressures of 3,000 psi, except for the 15 cubic foot pony bottle which has a service pressure of 2015.

P0000 — The tank's individual serial number is a ltter followed by a four or five digit number. Luxfer uses different letters to designate the size of the cylinder. Thus, the P designates that the tank is an 80 cubic foot cylinder; a Y indicates 71.2 cubic feet; an R indicates 50 cubic feet; and a KK is stamped on all 15 cubic foot tanks. All of the letters are followed by the individual serial number of the tank, which can be used for identification purposes.

LUXFER — indicates the name of the manufacturer, which appears after the serial number of the tank.

8 A 82 — indicates the month and the year of the first hydrostatic test, (August of 1982). The symbol in between the date is the symbol of the agency that has inspected the tank. Authorized Testing of California inspects Luxfer tanks, and their company symbol is a big A with a T inside.

STEEL TANK

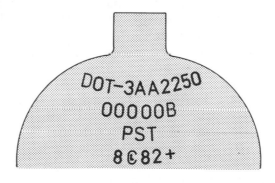

Steel Tanks — Most steel scuba tanks currently manufactured in the U.S. come from Pressed Steel in Wisconsin. The symbols on the neck of a steel tank indicate the following information about the tank:

DOT — denotes the regulating agency, DEPARTMENT OF TRANS-PORTATION, indicating the steel tank meets U.S. specifications.

3AA — denotes the alloy of which the tank is made, which is chrome molybdenum steel. (Older tanks that are stamped with 3A are made of carbon steel.)

2250 — The service pressure of the cylinder appears after the alloy designation. On steel 94.6 cubic foot tanks the pressure in pounds per square inch (psi) is 3,000; on 71.2 cubic foot tanks the pressure is 2250; and on 50's, the cylinder pressure is 1,800 psi.

00000B — The tank's individual serial number appears on the second line of the tank. This may be just numbers, or both letters and numbers. Yours is the only tank that has been issued this number, so keep it recorded somewhere for identification purposes.

PST — This is the symbol for Pressed Steel, which is the manufacturer of the tank. (Some older tanks may also bear the name or initials of the company that sells or distributes the tank.)

8 C1 82 + — Indicates the month and year of the first hydro test, in this case, August of 1982. The symbol or initials of the inspection agency appears between them. In each successive hydro test, the mark of the testing agency will be found in this position.

+ — New tanks will usually have a plus sign after the date of the hydro, indicating that the tank is strong enough to be filled to 10% above the working pressure stamped on the cylinder. This plus will only appear on steel tanks, and never on aluminum ones. Steel tanks are given this plus usually only the first time they are hydro tested.

Other Tanks — Foreign made tanks that are imported into the U.S. can be used here only if they conform to DOT specifications, although they do not need to have DOT stamped on them.

There are a number of tanks manufactured each year that may differ in size or working pressure from the commonly used steel and aluminum tanks. It is important to always check and adhere to the working pressure stamped on the neck of these tanks. If you run across an oddly shaped or sized tank that you are unfamiliar with, always check the hydro testing information before using it to make sure it is safe, or inquire at your local dive shop for more information regarding the tank.

The scuba industry is constantly innovating new changes and designs in scuba diving equipment. One unusual tank that may appear on the market in the near future is a stainless steel tank that is just under 2 feet tall and weighs about 23 pounds and will hold 89 cubic feet of air with a service pressure of 4000 psi. Design researchers of the future eventually hope to find a way to replace the large and cumbersome scuba cylinders that we use with smaller, lighter and more manageable ones.

Tank Valves

The two major types of tank valves commercially used for scuba cylinders today are known as the *K Valve* and the *J Valve*. The primary function of both types of valves is to regulate the air flow to and from the tank through an on/off control knob. The only difference between the two types of valves is that the *J Valve* incorporates an additional warning mechanism designed to let the diver know when his air supply in the tank is becoming low.

OPERATION OF A J VALVE

The warning device, or "reserve" mechanism, on the J Valve is activated by tank pressure through the spring tension inside the valve. As the tank pressure drops to 300 psi, the spring starts moving the valve slowly towards the closed position. The resistance to the air flow is felt by the diver as breathing becomes increasingly difficult. The diver then activates the J reserve lever by pulling it. This overrides the spring pressure, opening the valve and allowing the diver to freely use the remaining air in the tank.

The spring tension on most J Valves is normally set to be activated once the tank pressure drops to 300 psi. However, on one or two of the J Valves currently on the market, the spring tension may be adjusted to a spring tension pressure of 600 psi, providing for a larger reserve supply of air. This may be desirable during deep dives, or when using a crossover valve assembly on double tanks.

The J Valve reserve mechanism is only a warning system, designed to alert the diver that he is low on air. It does not provide extra air through a hidden auxiliary system, nor does it provide any more air than the tank normally holds. When the J Valve becomes actuated, the diver should be aware that his air supply is low, and act accordingly.

TROUBLESHOOTING RESERVE MECHANISMS

If you dive with a J valve and depend upon its warning mechanism to notify you when your air supply is becoming low, it is imperative that the valve function correctly when needed. Note the following ways in which a reserve mechanism can fail the unsuspecting diver, as well as corrective measures to be taken.

1. If the J valve has been accidentally activated to the on position during or before the dive, there will be no reserve supply of air when breathing becomes difficult. Before you enter the water, make sure that you and your buddy check each other's reserve valves to insure that they are in the "ready" position. Watch out for entangling kelp strands or rocky ledges that may accidentally trip the mechanism while underwater.

BASIC J VALVE DESIGN (Cross Section)

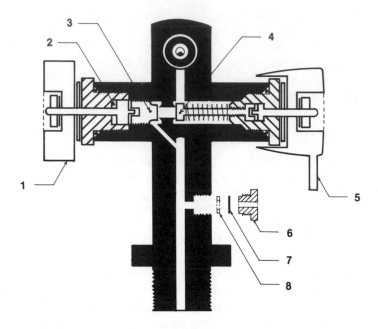

1. On/Off Wheel 2. Packing 3. Valve Seat 4. J Valve Seat 5. J Valve Knob. 6. Burst Disc Plug 7. Burst Disc 8. Packing.

2. Make sure you know how to pull the reserve mechanism when needed. Attach a "pull rod" to the lever to facilitate finding and operating the valve.

3. Always put the reserve lever *down* when filling your tank with air. The J valve can be easily damaged by attempting to fill a tank with the reserve lever in the "ready" position. If the reserve lever is left "up" when filling double tanks, only one tank will be filled.

4. Avoid weakening the spring by storing the tank with the spring under an activated position for an extended period of time. If the spring becomes weak, it will take less pressure to activate it and may not go off until the tank pressure is somewhere below 300 psi. The J valve should be stored with the reserve mechanism in the "ready" position in order to reduce tension on the spring.

5. To check your J valve for proper operation, place the reserve lever in the "ready" position (closed) as you normally would before your dive.

Continue your dive until the resistance is noticed, indicating the J valve should be opened. Then, while opening the J valve or pulling it to the "down" position, note the reading on your submersible pressure gauge. If the pressure is below 300 psi, the spring may be weak and may have to be replaced.

6. A faulty reserve mechanism can also be caused by a blown seat inside the valve. A rubber seat can be dislodged or "blown" as the sudden burst of air rushes past it when the reserve is pulled on or when the tank is being filled. A J valve with a metal seat, however, will not have this problem.

REMOVING A VALVE FROM A TANK

Tank valves should not be removed unless the proper tools are available, as removing the valve incorrectly can ruin or damage the valve. Most divers never have occasion to remove their tank valves themselves, as they usually have access to professional facilities where the valve can be removed with special tools.

However, in the event that you are traveling by plane, and must remove the valve for a customs inspection or for transporting the scuba cylinder, you will want to know how to safely remove your valve from your tank. The following procedure is recommended for removing a tank valve.

1. Drain the air from the tank, taking care to let the air escape very slowly from the tank. It is best to leave the tank low after the last dive, and then breathe out the remainder of the air with your regulator. To insure that the tank is completely drained of air, operate all valves, actuate the J valve back and forth and check for any escaping air.

2. Install the scuba cylinder in a chain or strap vice to hold the tank securely in place. If a square-jawed vice is used, the tank can become distorted or the coating can be damaged. The best vice is one that conforms to the shape of the cylinder without damaging it.

3. If the valve has wrench flats specifically designed for removing the valve, place a large wrench across the flats, using one hand to hold the wrench in place and the other to turn the wrench. Loosen the valve very carefully, taking care not to gouge the tank or the valve.

4. If the valve has no wrench flats, place a wide-jawed wrench across the face of the valve opening. Holding the wrench in place, loosen the valve carefully, making sure the wrench has a tight fit across the valve so as not to distort the valve. *Never* use the wrench on the sides of the valve, as it may crush or elongate the O-ring groove at the outlet of the valve. If the wrench is too narrow, it may dig into the valve.

5. If any leaks start to occur while removing the valve, *stop immediately,* until the air stops leaking out of the tank. Sometimes a residual amount

left in the tank will cause a slight stream of air. Proceed when the air stops leaking.

6. If when attempting to remove the valve the valve loosens a turn or so and then becomes tight again, stop immediately. This is usually an indication that the threads are starting to gaul. The valve should be removed only by a qualified repairman or a hydro facility, as further attempts at removal will destroy the threads in the tank, rendering the tank useless. This problem is most common when removing valves from aluminum tanks.

7. On some older tank valves, you may find a reducer adaptor installed to allow 1/2'' tapered valves to be threaded into one-inch tapered tank necks. These should be removed with the valve assembly, and not separately.

8. After the valve has been removed, inspect the valve thoroughly, and always give the tank a *visual inspection* anytime the valve has been removed from the tank.

TAPERED THREAD VALVE

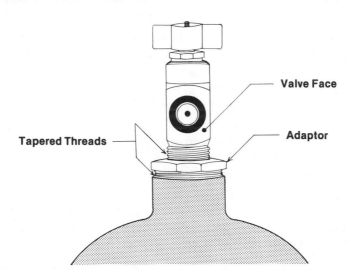

Valve Face

Tapered Threads

Adaptor

TO INSPECT A TANK VALVE

Anytime a valve is removed from a tank, it should be carefully inspected. All valves manufactured today are O-ring seal type valves, but some older models may use a pipe-threaded valve. If you have an older type pipe-threaded valve on the tank, take note of special handling and maintenance procedures peculiar to this type of valve.

The proper procedure for inspecting a tank valve is as follows:

1. Inspect the valve for possible signs of corrosion. If corrosion is detected, it may be removed by using a warm solution of 50% white vinegar and water. Soak the valve for about ten minutes. After soaking, the parts must be thoroughly rinsed with fresh water, then dried, using a low pressure steam of air, if possible.

2. Also inspect the valve knobs for signs of bending, cracking or distortion.

3. Inspect the O-ring seat outlet of the valve for possible signs of cracks, nicks, or distortion. The threads in the valve should also be carefully inspected for possible gouges or corrosion.

4. Pipe Thread Valves: Remove all teflon tape before inspecting and reinstalling the valve on the tank. Never use teflon tape on O-ring sealed valves. The O-ring is the seal, not the tape.

Note: Some newly manufactured tank valves have a small dent or "upset" in the inner O-ring land. This is designed to bleed off high pressure air from the O-ring cavity. (It is intentional, and not a manufacturer's defect.) The purpose of this small dent is to enable you to remove your regulator more easily and to prevent the O-ring from blowing out when the regulator is removed from the tank valve.

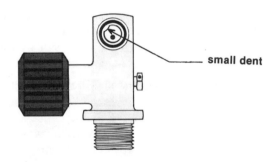

Tank valve showing manufacturer designed O-ring land upset, or small dent.

TO INSTALL A TANK VALVE

Before installing a tank valve, make sure the tank has been given a visual inspection. Check to insure that the neck threads are clean and in good condition both inside the tank and on the valve assembly.

Pipe-Thread Valves — All teflon tape should be removed and new tape installed. One wrapping of the circumference around the threads will suffice for sealing the tank. Do not use multiple wraps. Install the valve a good two to three turns very carefully and gently by hand only. Never use a wrench to force it in, as it is very easy to strip the threads in the valve. Make sure the valve is threaded properly.

After insuring that the valve is positioned properly, it should be tightened with a wrench until it is snug, but not so tight that it will make future removal difficult.

O-Ring Seal Valves — Teflon tape should never be used on O-ring seal valves, as particles of the tape can become dislodged and prevent the O-ring from sealing properly. Make sure the tank neck is clean, and that no corrosion is evident. Rub a small amount of NON-TOXIC silicone on the O-ring before installing. On aluminum tanks a special moly lubricant is used before installing the tank valve.

Install the valve on the tank very carefully by hand, taking care to position the valve properly. Tighten the valve by hand until the O-ring is snug against the seat. Then the valve should be tightened up with a wrench, taking care not to overtighten, since the O-ring seals the valve, not the tightness of the threads.

Anytime the valve is removed, a new O-ring should be installed on the valve to tank seal. After reinstalling the valve properly, fill the tank with air very slowly, paying attention to the seal to check for leaks. This should be done while the tank is submersed in water in a fill tank.

TANK VALVE MAINTENANCE

Washing — The tank valve should be rinsed after each dive with fresh water. When washing the valve, it should be washed with the regulator installed and pressurized. The valve should be open. Direct the flow of water in the on/off knobs and the J valve knob. Salt or foreign material left around these knobs can cause leakage by damaging the seals.

Operating — When turning the air on and off, always turn the valve handle all the way out gently until it reaches its outer stop, then turn it back slightly. Never turn it hard enough to damage the valve seat, as this could eventually cause a leak around the nylon or teflon washer inside.

When turning the air off, always do so gently. Don't exert force to twist the knob too far. It should be closed just tight enough to stop the flow of air, but never tightened down to excess. If tightened excessively, damage to the seat in the valve can result, causing the valve to seal improperly.

Handling — Remember: The valve is the weakest part of the tank. It is not protected by any type of covering. Take care not to drop the tank, forcibly causing the valve to become damaged, distorted, or even snapped off. When traveling with tanks, make sure the valve is protected from being bumped or banged around.

Attaching a Regulator — Always open the valve momentarily with just a slight movement before attaching the regulator. This will blow away any moisture or foreign particles from the valve opening. Then attach the regulator, making sure that the inlet O-ring between the tank valve and regulator housing is in place and in good condition.

Lubrication — Never use any type of lubricants in the tank valve. Oil, grease and silicone products may produce harmful vapors to breathe. However, a small amount of silicone lubricant may be used on the valve to tank O-rings, taking care not to spray or apply silicone to the valve or tank.

Tank Pressure Indicator — Some valves have a tank pressure indicator on the back of them. This is a small pin that moves and indicates whether the tank is empty, half full or full. The pressure indicator pin is sealed with an O-ring. If any sand or salt is left around the pin, it may damage the O-ring, causing it to leak around the base of the pressure indicator pin. This area should always be carefully inspected for foreign particles and rinsed thoroughly after a dive.

TWIN VALVE ASSEMBLIES

There are two types of twin valve assemblies. One is the twin manifold type, which is made specifically for double tanks and can only be used on twin assemblies. The other is the crossover type, which incorporates the original valves on the tanks in a twin assembly. Tanks on crossover assemblies can be easily removed and used as single tanks, with no modifications required.

Twin Manifold — The twin manifold incorporates a valve that connects two tanks together. The assembly has one separate on/off valve, which turns both tanks on and off simultaneously. If there is a reserve lever, it is connected to only one of the tanks, and is then set at 500 or 600 psi.

Each cylinder will have its own burst disc assembly. Twin tanks should always be carried by the backpacks or handled as close to the tank valves as possible. Never carry them at the center of the manifold, as the stress can break the assembly or cause it to become bent or distorted.

Twin Crossover — On the crossover assembly, a special crossover bar connects two separate tanks together using the valves that are already on each tank. Both valves will have their own burst disc assemblies. If J valves are used with crossover assemblies, you should use one that is adjustable to 600 psi. Then, when you trip the reserve mechanism, the air distributes evenly in both tanks and both tanks will contain 300 psi. Only use tanks with the same psi ratings.

If the J valve is set to 300 psi on twin crossover assemblies, the tank with the J valve will empty half of its air into the other tank when the reserve mechanism is tripped at 300 psi. Thus, instead of giving you 300 psi of reserve air, you will actually only have 150 psi left. It is usually not a good idea to set up a crossover system with a J valve on each tank. It is inconvenient to have to actuate both of them at once, and either one of them could become bumped or tripped accidentally.

Avoid getting water in the crossover assembly. Water can enter the valve or the crossover inlet, and it can fill the entire crossover with water. Since the entire crossover can fill, opening one valve will just purge out half of the water, and half of the water will stay inside, going back and forth from one valve to the other. To properly purge the crossover assembly of water, it is best to remove it from the tanks, then blow out the moisture using only one of the tanks. Because of the problem with water entering the crossover assembly, tanks are susceptible to accumulating moisture in the interior.

TWIN CROSSOVER MANIFOLD

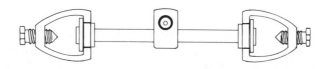

TWIN MANIFOLD ASSEMBLY

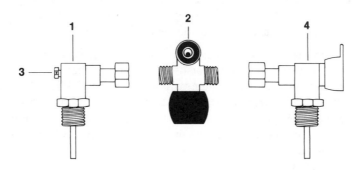

1. Elbow Assembly 2. On/Off Valve Body 3. Burst Disc Assembly 4. Elbow Assembly with J Valve.

$1\frac{2}{3} = \frac{5}{3}$ of normal pressure in aluminum tank

BURST DISC ASSEMBLIES

The burst disc assembly in the tank valve can also be referred to as the over pressure relief assembly. The assembly consists of a gasket, a burst disc, and a blow out plug. The burst disc is designed to rupture, allowing air to vent from the tank, when the pressure inside the tank becomes high enough to rupture the disc, thus preventing the tank itself from exploding.

There are two types of blow plugs used in burst disc assemblies:

Metal-backed plug — This type of blow plug incorporates a piece of metal or a metal plug behind the burst disc. In case of overheating, the metal plug will melt, enabling the air to flow out of the tank. A major problem with using metal-backed plugs is that *both* high pressure and high temperature are needed to cause the disc to blow. Thus, even if the tank is grossly overfilled at room temperature, the metal-backed plug would not provide the necessary relief for the tank, unless the temperature were also high enough. This type of plug can also blow very easily when subjected to overheating alone. Metal-backed plugs are generally not recommended for sport divers, and should be replaced with the non-backed type whenever possible.

Non-backed plug — The non-backed burst disc retaining plug is recommended for sportdiving purposes. It has a hole drilled through the center, and is placed over the burst disc and screwed into place. This plug operates on pressure, so if the tank becomes overpressurized, the disc will burst, allowing the air to escape from the tank. An increase in the air temperature inside the tank will also cause an increase in pressure, since hot air will expand, causing the disc to burst.

An additional safety feature has recently been added to the non-backed retaining plug, and is considered the safest to use. Instead of allowing all of the air to vent through a single center-drilled hole, the air is vented through two holes that are drilled at 90° to the center. The double side-drilled holes serve to counter balance the force of the escaping air should the burst disc rupture, and the tank will not whirl dangerously out of control.

Maintenance — Anytime you purchase a tank, or change a valve, always check to insure that the proper burst disc is used on the tank valve. Every valve must have a good burst disc assembly. After years of use, normal flexing and corrosion will cause the disc to fail at normal pressure and temperature. When replacing the burst disc assembly, do not interchange old parts with new ones. Always replace the gasket, burst disc and blow plug at the same time with new parts.

If any air leaks around the burst disc assembly, drain the tank slowly of its air, then remove the disc plug. Inspect the gasket, the disc and the plug for any holes or defects, also insuring that it is the correct burst disc for your tank. Replace the burst disc assembly, if necessary. Anytime leaking is noticed, the tank should be drained of air, and the burst disc assembly

Older style burst disc retaining plugs (both the metal-backed type and the non-backed type with a center-drilled hole) should be replaced with the newer non-backed plug featuring two side-drilled holes (see far right). The side-drilled holes are a safety feature that prevents the tank from propelling out of control should the disc assembly burst.

should be removed from the valve and inspected.

When washing the tank valve assembly, direct a stream of water to the burst disc assembly, to remove any salt or foreign particles that may have accumulated.

Malfunctions — The burst disc assembly should blow out and release the air in the tank anytime the pressure inside the tank increases to the pressure that falls within the burst range of the disc. The following chart indicates the proper burst range of psi pressure that corresponds to the working pressure of the scuba cylinder:

Cylinder Working Pressure	PSI Burst Range
1800 PSI	2400—2700
2015 PSI	2700—3000
2250 PSI	2850—3375
3000 PSI	3960—4400

Anytime the burst disc assembly is replaced in your scuba tank, always insure that you select the correct burst disc assembly corresponding with the working pressure of your scuba cylinder. Using a burst disc on a cylinder with a lower working pressure than that indicated for the burst range could cause damage and bodily injury.

The burst disc assembly can also blow out and allow air to escape from the tank through improper functioning, such as when the disc has not been cleaned properly or when corrosion has set in. With severe corrosion, over a period of time, the burst disc could blow out anytime. This could be potentially dangerous in any number of diving situations.

With normal use and time, the burst disc assembly will weaken and may become worn out. With a constant increase and decrease in pressure through emptying and filling the tank, the disc will undergo a constant flexing that can wear it out over a period of time. It is always a good idea to inspect the burst disc assembly before every diving season, or at least once a year, and to simply replace it with new components. Replacement kits are inexpensive, and can be obtained through professional dive shops.

BACKPACK ASSEMBLIES

There are a variety of backpack assemblies on the market from which the diver may choose to suit his particular diving needs.

Contour Pack — As its name indicates, this backpack is designed to contour to the back of the diver. It may be made of plastic, or of metal with a vinyl plastic coating.

Flat Pack — This is the most popular modern day pack for diving tanks. It is constructed of molded plastic, and is generally hollow inside.

Hawaiian backpack — This backpack uses hooks, instead of straps, that fit over the shoulders of the diver. The only straps on the pack are the waist straps which are used to hold the tank on.

Canvas strap pack — This type of backpack is used only on twin assemblies. There is no pack assembly involved. Instead, straps that are attached directly to the bands that hold the twin tanks together hold the tanks in place on the back.

Buoyancy Compensator Backpack — A recent innovation in backpack designs incorporates velcro/webbing tank bands as an integral part of the BC unit. This eliminates the need for a separate backpack.

Whatever type of backpack setup you use for your scuba tanks, it should be designed to position the tank comfortably and securely, and should also be comfortable in any position in the water.

There are two types of attachments that hold the tanks in place to facilitate removal and placement of the tanks on the backpack:

1. Cam Pack — also called a quick disconnect pack and has provisions for adjusting the tank band, allowing for quick installation and removal of the tank through a latch assembly. One assembly will generally fit any size tank. Cam packs are made of either stainless steel or a combination of velcro and webbing.

2. Fixed Adjustment Pack — This is the least expensive type of attachment. It is installed on one tank at a time, adjusted to securely fit that tank size, and is not easily interchangeable without a moderate amount of readjustment to fit another tank.

TWIN ASSEMBLY BACKPACKS

Whenever using twin tanks, always install them in a twin-banded pack. This will prevent "diamond shaping" of the tanks which could cause the manifold to bend or become distorted.

To Assemble Twin Tanks — In order to make up a set of twin tanks from your single tanks, first insure that the tanks are the same size with the same style neck and same type of tank boots. They must also have the same pressure rating. Set them upright on the floor and measure them both from the floor to the tank neck or valve opening, to insure equal height. This is critical for both the twin manifold or crossover assembly.

Double check your measurements. In the twin manifold set-up, just the height of the tank from the floor to the top of the tank should be checked. In the crossover assembly, you will have to insure that the openings in the valve of each tank are of the same height.

Install the valve assembly. Slide the backpack over the tanks. Lay the tanks down on a flat surface, so that they lie parallel. Then install the center section of the twin manifold and tighten it by hand. For crossover assemblies, place the valve faces towards each other and install the crossover. Tighten until snug. Stand the tanks up, and adjust the height of the backpack for your needs.

Now tighten the bands alternately, first the top, then the bottom. Keep the space between the tanks equal all the way down. Don't overtighten. Check to insure that they sit level on the ground after the backpack is installed.

On quick disconnect packs, or cam packs, periodically lubricate the cam locks and the band size adjustment mechanism with a light coat of oil. This will keep the moving parts operating freely for adjustments.

CARE AND MAINTENANCE

When choosing a backpack for your tanks, insure that the fittings are made of non-corrosive metal and that the straps are of a material that will not rot easily. The backpack should be sturdily constructed. Thin, plastic packs become brittle and may eventually crack.

Some backpacks are made of metal that is covered with a coating of vinyl plastic. These should always be washed thoroughly and inspected around the area where the tank band attaches to the backpack for any signs of corrosion that may occur as a result of the contact of dissimilar metals. A light spraying with a coat of WD-40 before storing will help to prevent corrosion.

Never tighten a tank excessively on a backpack, so as to cause the screws to be pulled out through the backpack, or to otherwise cause cracking and distortion. Cam locks should be lubricated with a light coat of oil after washing and drying. Don't use grease or silicone, as these will attract sand and other particles. Also lubricate the band size adjustment mechanism.

The most trouble-free packs are the ones that have a metal tank band running completely through the backpack and around the tank, thus securing them together without the use of extra hardware. They are one solid unit, and holes do not have to be drilled into the backpack. Whatever type of backpack you use, make sure the tank is installed securely in the pack before each dive. Pick up the tank and pack and shake it up and down, insuring that nothing moves or slips.

To tighten a tank band which may have become stretched, you can simply install a new neoprene band liner inside the tank band, to make the tank secure again. Never leave any screws sticking out of the backpack. These can dig into your back or wetsuit, or may catch on something else.

When washing the quick disconnect attachment, always remove it from the tank and rinse the entire assembly, paying attention to the fastenings, snaps and buckles. Remove any sand or salt particles, and use a stiff brush to remove sand from velcro attachments.

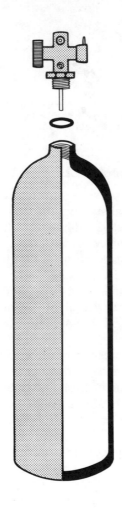

Scuba Regulators

The type of underwater breathing apparatus that sportdivers use almost exclusively today is referred to as open-circuit scuba. Compressed air from a high pressure cylinder flows through a regulator assembly in a series of intricate valves and chambers. The regulator reduces the high pressure air in the tank to the ambient pressure surrounding the diver's lungs, thus making the air from the cylinder safe and breathable for the diver. A regulator provides the diver with air upon demand, and automatically controls the flow of air to the diver.

The regulator assembly is an important component of the diver's life support system, but it is also often the most neglected. Most regulator repairmen generally agree that poor maintenance procedures and a lack of fundamental knowledge about regulators are the prime factors leading to regulator malfunctions. While regulators may look like very simple gadgets, their internal mechanisms are designed with very close tolerances and fine clearances that can be easily disturbed by outside contaminants and improper handling.

TYPES OF REGULATORS

There are several types of scuba regulators that a sportdiver may encounter. They are differentiated according to the number of stages and hoses incorporated in their design. The stages on a regulator refer to the number of reductions in pressure that the air stored in the tank will have to undergo before it is reduced sufficiently for the diver to breathe. Most regulators today reduce the air pressure in two stages. Although you might run across a one-stage regulator on a rare occasion, this type is no longer in common use.

Two stage regulators are available in two different styles, the double hose and the single hose version. Double hose regulators, however, are becoming outdated, and are rapidly falling into disuse. Leading manufacturers are discontinuing their production, and it is becoming increasingly difficult to obtain spare parts for this type of regulator. The most commonly used type of scuba regulator today is the single hose, two stage regulator.

Single Hose Regulators — The single hose regulator is designed to supply the diver with air from a high pressure cylinder through two different stages of pressure reduction. The first pressure reduction is accomplished in the first stage of the regulator, which is mounted on the tank. The first stage reduces the tank pressure to an intermediate pressure between 110 and 185 psi above ambient pressure. (The pressure rating may vary with individual regulators.)

A single, small diameter hose then connects the first stage to a second stage which further reduces the air pressure to ambient pressure. The second stage is connected to the diver's mouthpiece, and provides breathable air at the mouthpiece for inhalation by the diver. Exhaled air is then exhausted from the second stage directly into the water.

Double Hose Regulators — Although double hose regulators are fast becoming museum pieces, they are still preferred by some divers and may make an occasional appearance in sportdiving circles. The double hose regulator incorporates both pressure reduction stages in the same housing. This housing is one large container that mounts directly onto the high pressure cylinder valve behind the diver's head. Large diameter, corrugated hoses made of rubber extend from each side of the housing to the diver's mouthpiece. One of the low pressure hoses provides the diver with breathable air from the reduction stages, while the other low pressure hose returns the diver's exhaled air back to the housing where it is exhausted into the water behind the diver's head.

Single Hose VS Double Hose — In the past, sportdivers could compare the advantages and disadvantages of using either a single hose or a double hose regulator, and center their selection around their own personal preferences. Overwhelmingly, however, sportdivers have opted for the single hose regulator.

The advantages contributing to the popularity currently enjoyed by the single hose regulator include the following:

1. Single hose regulators are generally less expensive to purchase than double hose models, and the cost of maintenance is less due to the durability of the hose and the internal working parts. Spare parts are also widely available.

2. Single hose regulators provide less drag in the water, due to the smaller diameter hose made possible by moving the second stage to the diver's mouthpiece.

3. The low pressure differential diaphragm is located near the same level as the diver's lungs, where it will provide a more controlled flow of air to the diver's lungs.

4. Divers generally find a single hose regulator easier to operate and adjust to than a double hose model. It also provides a greater freedom of head movement and maneuverability for the diver, due to the decreased size of the hose.

5. Single hose regulators are easier to purge or clear, should it come out of the mouth or fill with water. It may also be easier to buddy breathe with in an emergency, since most divers are accustomed to single hose regulators.

Proponents of double hose regulators generally choose the double hose version for some of the following advantages:

1. The mouthpiece of a double hose regulator is light weight, since the second stage is located elsewhere, and may not be as tiring to the diver's jaws during long periods of immersion underwater.

2. Since the exhaust bubbles escape behind the neck, there are no annoying and noisy bubbles rushing up past your ears and face. Underwater photographers often prefer double hose regulators for this reason, since it places the distracting bubbles further away from their photo subjects.

3. Double hose regulators provide easier exhalation efforts for the diver, since the exhaust valve is located slightly higher than the mouthpiece, and the exhaled air will seek the higher level by itself.

4. Double hose regulators are not as vulnerable to freezing up in very cold water temperatures as are single hose regulators. This is largely due to their internal construction, which keeps water out of the intake hose and out of the regulator assembly itself. This assures that water never touches the first stage diaphragm, and the internal mechanical parts and openings are not prone to being clogged and jammed by ice particles that may build up.

Durability and Ease of Operation — In terms of durability and ease of operation, the single hose regulator clearly prevails over its double hose counterpart. Barring only some new and heretofor untried design improvement by equipment engineers, the single hose regulator seems likely to dominate the diving industry for years to come. Today's single hose regulators are extremely reliable pieces of equipment, and manufacturers adhere to rigorous standards of production and inspection to insure the highest operational safety standards possible.

Use and Maintenance: *Caution* — A scuba regulator is a sophisticated piece of equipment that supports life underwater. A regulator should never be used by anyone who has not completed a basic scuba course from a qualified instructor, or who is not under close supervision from a qualified instructor. Physical injury and fatalities have occured in cases involving inexperienced divers using scuba equipment.

Do not disassemble your regulator yourself. *Only* qualified repairmen with the proper tools and knowledge should perform essential repairs and overhauls on regulators. Also, make sure your regulator is serviced regularly by a repairman who is familiar with your particular type of regulator assembly. Your regulator should be serviced at least once a year by a professional technician, and more frequently if heavily used.

HOW A REGULATOR WORKS

The following section will pertain exclusively to single hose regulators. While some of the operating principles and mechanisms are essentially the same in both types of regulators, a detailed discussion of double hose regulators has little value for the modern sportdiver, whose chances of ever coming across one are practically nonexistent.

Automatic Air Supply — The single hose regulator is a combination of two demand valve mechanisms which reduce the high pressure air stored in the tank to a breathable, or ambient, air pressure stored at the mouthpiece. A properly functioning regulator will correctly regulate the airflow and will automatically reduce the high pressure air to ambient pressure upon demand, or when the diver inhales.

The automatic pressure reduction that takes place in both stages of the regulator should occur without any abnormal amount of exertion on the part of the diver when he demands air. It has been found that high resistance to breathing affects divers both physically and psychologically. A well maintained and routinely serviced regulator should perform well under normal diving conditions, with a minimum amount of inhalation and exhalation effort required of the diver.

In the relatively short history of the design development of regulators, several types of valve mechanisms have been designed to reduce and control the air flow to the diver. Some of the valves have fallen into disuse today, while other types are still commonly used, and still others are recent innovations.

First Stage Valves — The first stage of the regulator is the assembly that attaches to the tank valve. Its function is to reduce the high pressure air from the tank to an intermediate pressure before it flows through the regulator hose to the second stage located at the diver's mouthpiece. This is accomplished through a specially designed internal valve. Regulator first stage valves fall into two basic types: balanced valves and unbalanced valves.

Before 1961, all U.S. made single hose regulators used only unbalanced valves. Today, most regulators being manufactured in the U.S. incorporate a balanced first stage valve. And most regulator technicians generally agree that it is preferable to have a balanced valve in the first stage of the regulator.

The basic difference between an unbalanced and a balanced valve is that a balanced valve will keep the hose pressure steady regardless of changes in tank pressure. In an unbalanced valve, the valve inside the first stage is affected by the change in pressure of the incoming air from the tank, resulting in a change in the air pressure leaving the first stage as well.

Thus, when a tank pressure changes as the air is drained from the tank, the air pressure in the hose is affected by the change, which alters the pressure at the mouthpiece. Breathing could thus be easier or harder, depending upon the air pressure in the tank, when an unbalanced valve is used in the first stage.

There are four basic types of valves utilized in the first stage assembly: 1) *Unbalanced Diaphragm Valve* 2) *Unbalanced Piston Valve* 3) *Balanced Piston Valve* 4) *Balanced Diaphragm Valve*. A brief discussion of each of these types of valves will give a general idea of their design, function and differences.

1)*Unbalanced Diaphragm Valve* — This valve is also referred to as an upstream first stage valve, since the valve seat is located on the upstream or high pressure side of the valve. As the diver inhales, a diaphragm flexes inward, pushing on a rod which causes the valve to open. Air flow is thus provided to the diver. The valve closes when the diaphragm is returned to its relaxed position as the pressure builds up in the intermediate chamber and reaches a pre-determined level.

A major disadvantage of this type of valve (characteristic of all unbalanced first stage valves) is that the high pressure air acts directly on the valve, effecting the opening and closing of the valve.

To compensate for this effect, the valve opening is often made smaller, but this in turn results in a reduced flow of air. This type of valve may be found in some older type regulators, but it has largely been phased out, and is rarely found on today's modern regulators.

DIAPHRAGM UNBALANCED FIRST STAGE

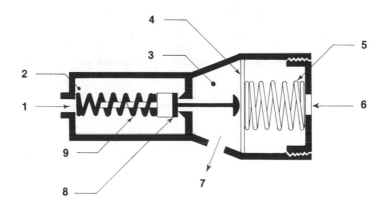

1. High Pressure Air 2. High Pressure Air Chamber 3. Intermediate Chamber 4. Diaphragm 5. Diaphragm Balance Spring 6. Ambient Water Pressure 7. Air to Second Stage 8. Valve and Seat Assembly 9. Valve Balance Spring.

2) *Unbalanced Piston Valve* — This valve operates by the opposing forces of the intermediate pressure and the main balance spring of the regulator. When the diver inhales, the intermediate pressure drops, causing the main spring pressure to move the piston towards the low pressure side. When the piston moves, it takes the valve off its seat, allowing air from the tank to enter and causing the intermediate pressure to rise. This pressure increase overcomes the main spring pressure, causing the piston to move to the closed position, thus closing the valve so no more air can enter from the tank.

Since this is an *unbalanced* valve, the valve is affected by the pressure change in the air entering from the tank. As tank pressure decreases, the valve will alter its sensitivity. Thus, as tank pressure drops, breathing will become more labored toward the lower pressure. Although these types of first stage valves are gradually being replaced with *balanced* valves, there are still quite a few of them around today in numberous types of regulators.

UNBALANCED PISTON FIRST STAGE

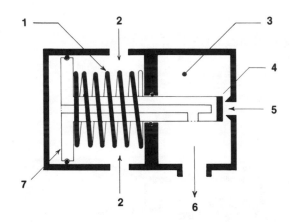

1. Balance Spring 2. Ambient Water Pressure 3. Intermediate Chamber 4. Valve and Seat Assembly 5. High Pressure Air 6. Air to Second Stage 7. First Stage Piston

60

BALANCED PISTON FIRST STAGE

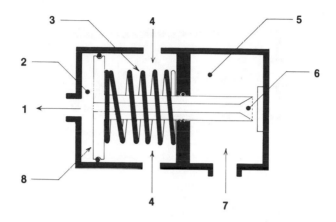

1. Air to Second Stage 2. Intermediate Chamber 3. Balance Spring 4. Ambient Water Pressure 5. high Pressure Air Chamber 6. Valve and Seat Assembly 7. High Pressure Air 8. Piston Assembly.

3) *Balanced Piston Valve* — This type of valve operates in the same manner as the unbalanced piston valve, except that when the piston moves causing the valve to open, the valve is not influenced by the high pressure air coming from the tank. Thus, the valve will open and close unaffected by the change in the tank pressure. This will provide a more consistent and smoother flow of regulated air to the second stage. With piston valves, two vital O-ring seals inside the first stage are subject to malfunction if damaged by sand or salt crystals.

4) *Balanced Diaphragm Valve* — The operation of the balanced diaphragm valve is essentially the same as the balanced piston valve, except that a flexible diaphragm is used to push the air valve open, instead of a metal piston. This valve was developed to eliminate the effects of the changes in the high pressure cylinder air on the first stage valve. Since the valve stem extends through the high pressure chamber into the intermediate air chamber that flows through the hose, the high pressure air from the cylinder can not exert a closing force on the valve stem. The air pressure in the intermediate chamber acts to help balance the forces acting on the valve stem.

61

DIAPHRAGM BALANCED FIRST STAGE

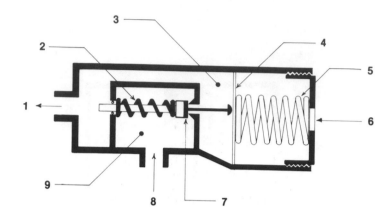

1. Air to Second Stage 2. Valve Balance Spring 3. Intermediate Chamber 4. Diaphragm 5. Balance Spring 6. Ambient Water Pressure 7. Valve and Seat Assembly 8. High Pressure Air 9. High Pressure Air Chamber

Second Stage Valves — Most regulators manufactured today incorporate the use of down stream valves in the second stage. This means that the valve seat is situated on the down stream or after side of the valve assembly, and opens with the flow of air rather than against it. This is an important design feature, since it allows the intermedate air pressure to assist in opening the valve. Thus, if the first stage valve should malfunction, the high pressure air would not damage the hose or the second stage. Instead, it would force open the second stage valve and cause the regulator to free flow, while still providing air to the diver.

The two most popularly used types of valves in the second stage include the *Downstream Second Stage Valve* and the *Pilot Operated Valve.*

1) *Downstream Second Stage Valve* — This type of second stage valve incorporates the use of a return spring and a small lever to operate the valve. As the diver inhales, he lowers the pressure in the diaphragm pressure chamber. This causes the diaphragm to move inward and to depress the valve lever. This offseats the valve, causing the intermediate stage air to enter the second stage of the regulator. When the diver stops inhaling, the pressure increases from the air coming into the regulator and the diaphragm moves back out, stopping the flow of air. When the diver exhales, his exhausted air travels through the exhaust valve and out the exhaust port.

DOWNSTREAM SECOND STAGE VALVE

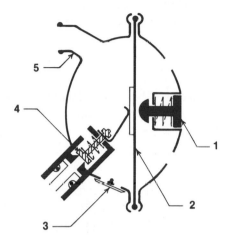

1. Purge Button
2. Diaphragm
3. Exhaust Valve
4. Second Stage
   Downstream Valve
5. Mouthpiece

2) *Pilot Operated Valve* — The pilot operated valve is one of the most recently developed types of valves used in regulator design. A pilot operated valve is actually made of two separate valves. The main valve regulates the air flow to the second stage, while the pilot valve is designed to open and close the main valve. As the diver inhales, the diaphragm bulges inward, causing a small lever to allow the pilot valve to move downward. As the pilot valve drops, air rushes into an intermediate chamber, causing a drop in air pressure, which in turn causes the main valve to open. Although this valve is usually classified as a balanced valve, a radical change in the air pressure in the hose could cause it to become unbalanced and begin to free flow.

Second Stage Exhaust Valves — The second stage exhaust valve in most regulators is a thin rubber or silicone "flap" that permits the discharge of exhaled gas from the second stage without permitting the entrance of water. Rubber exhaust valves will deteriorate and become stiff and brittle with age, so they need to be replaced periodically.

A deteriorating exhaust valve will take on a gummy appearance, and could stick to the regulator housing. Never treat the exhaust valve with any type of silicone or oil to preserve it. Silicone should never be sprayed into a regulator. It can cause thin rubber parts to warp, and may also be harmful to breathe. Silicone exhaust valves are not prone to deterioration, and will last longer than rubber ones.

HANDLING A REGULATOR

Use a separate bag for storing your regulator, to protect it from being banged around and from accumulating dust or other foreign matter. Regulator storage bags are available commercially through dive shops, or you can easily fabricate one yourself from a few scraps of neoprene. Get into the habit of covering your regulator every time it is put back into your diving gear bag.

Mounting a Regulator to a Tank

1. Before mounting the regulator to the tank, crack the tank valve slightly for a moment to blow out any moisture or contamination that may have accumulated in the air valve.

2. Inspect the tank valve inlet to insure that the tiny O-ring is in place, and that it is free of sand and dirt.

3. Attach the regulator, but don't overtighten the yoke screw. The tiny O-ring in the tank valve provides the proper seal, rather than the tighteness of the screw. As the air pressure is turned on, it forces the O-ring into place, making a pressurized seal.

4. With the second stage mounted to the tank valve securely, turn the air on slowly. Don't force the hand wheel past its full open position. This can wear down the O-ring seal inside the tank valve.

5. Check the air pressure in the tank. Make sure that the regulator is mounted with the hose falling over your right shoulder. Check to insure that the reserve lever is in the "up" position, if your tank has one. Breathe through the regulator to insure proper operation before entering the water.

Removing the Regulator from the Tank

1. Turn the air in the tank off. Then release the pressure that is trapped inside the regulator by either breathing the air out or by pushing the purge button.

2. Inspect the dust cap to make sure that it is free from sand and dirt, and it is dry. If necessary, dry it with a towel or with air from the tank, but be careful not to blow any water into the first stage high pressure air inlet. Then position the cap over the air inlet and gently tighten the yoke screw, just enough to make a watertight seal.

3. A dust cap should always be in place when the regulator is not in use. Use a solid, plastic dust cap with an O-ring, rather than a metal or a rubber one. A hollow plastic cap can crack easily and may leak. Metal dust caps are subject to electrolysis. And rubber caps may become distorted and fail to seal properly.

PREVENTATIVE MAINTENANCE

Cleaning — The most important maintenance procedure you can perform on your regulator is a complete, fresh water rinse immediately after, or within a few hours of your last dive. Even if you don't have a chance to rinse off your other equipment right away, try to see that your regulator gets a fresh water rinse as soon as possible, regardless of whether you have been diving in salt or fresh water.

If allowed to remain inside your regulator, dried salt crystals and sand particles can damage the precision parts inside. The chlorine and acids in swimming pools, as well as the mineral and alkaline deposits present in fresh water lakes and rivers can also cause corrosion and damage to many regulator components.

To properly rinse a regulator:

1. Make sure the dust cap is securely in place on the first stage air inlet and that it has a watertight seal.

2. Use warm, (but never hot) water to rinse or soak your regulator. This will dissolve into solution any dried salt crystals that may have accumulated in the interior.

3. Direct a low pressure stream of fresh water over the first stage, and allow it to run freely through any open ports. If your first stage uses a piston type valve, pay attention to rinsing all salt and sand out of the water chamber, as sand particles or salt buildup can interfere with the operation of the piston by causing damage to the piston O-ring.

4. Now rinse the second stage by directing a stream of fresh water into the mouthpiece and allowing it to exit through the exhaust tee. Flush water around and outside of the entire second stage. _Do not push the purge button,_ unless you are holding the hose and the first stage high above the second stage and away from the water.

5. Or, you can immerse the entire assembly in a tub of warm water, always assuring that the watertight dust cap is securely in place. This would be advisable if a period of time has lapsed after your dive without rinsing the regulator. Allow the regulator to soak for five to ten minutes, sloshing it around to loosen any stubborn particles.

6. The purge button should *never* be pushed while the regulator is completely immersed underwater. This opens the second stage valve, allowing water to flow through the hose and back into the interior of the first stage assembly.

7. Allow the regulator to dry thoroughly before storing it. Always dry it away from direct sunlight to protect the rubber parts.

Hoses — Hoses are often the most mistreated part of the regulator assembly, and are usually the most expensive to replace. They are fre-

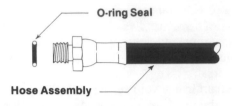

O-ring Seal

Hose Assembly

quently allowed to fray, chafe or rot, or are needlessly bent and stretched out of shape.

1. Always replace any hoses that become frayed, cut or badly chafed.

2. Use hose protectors (special rubber slip-on sleeves available at dive shops) to protect the area located next to the first stage that is subject to stress.

3. When rinsing the hose, slide the hose protectors back down the hose to rinse beneath them. This will protect the hose fitting from corrosion, and will insure that the hose can be removed easily without damage when needed. Allow the hose protector to dry thoroughly before sliding it back into position.

4. Sharp bends, kinks, and tight loops in the hoses can weaken and damage the hose. Air hoses are fabricated of nylon or cotton braid with inner and outer coatings of rubber. Unusual bending and distortion can weaken the integrity of the inner braiding. Don't hang a regulator by the first stage in such a manner so as to allow the hoses to bend.

5. Anytime hoses develop pin hole leaks, they should be replaced immediately. This is a sign that air is leaking through the lamination of the hose, and it will gradually become worse.

Fittings — Whenever working with hoses and fittings, always use the proper tools and proper size wrenches. This will prevent any galling or scratching from the wrench when the hose is removed. When removing or installing hoses onto the first stage of the regulator, support the first stage lightly in a soft-jawed vice to hold it securely.

1. Before installing a hose in the first stage, make sure that it is the correct hose (either high or low pressure), and install only in its respective port in the regulator. With most regulators, the port with the smallest internal hole is for the high pressure hose, and the port with the largest internal hole is for the low pressure hose. These are often labeled "HP" and "LP", respectively. However, on some regulators, these holes are of different sizes, making it almost impossible to accidentally attach a hose to the wrong port.

Attachment hoses must be installed in the proper port on the first stage of the regulator. The port with the smallest internal hole is for high pressure hoses, while the port with the larger internal hole is for low pressure hoses. These are often labeled accordingly with "HP" and "LP" to designate the respective ports.

2. If a leak is detected where the fitting attaches to the *First Stage,* this is often just a loose fitting, and can be solved by tightening the fitting. If the fitting is tight and the leak persists, remove the regulator from the tank. Next, remove the fitting from the first stage, remove the O-ring and install a new O-ring of the correct size. Reinstall the hose. Some regulators use "crush" gaskets, and these must be replaced with a like item. If the leak still persists, have the regulator serviced by a competent repairman.

3. If a leak is detected where the hose fitting is attached to the *Second Stage, Do Not Attempt To Tighten* this fitting unless you have the proper tools and knowledge to do so. This is a job best left for a regulator repairman, since damage to the second stage valve can result in some regulators if done incorrectly.

Lubrication — Never apply any type of lubricants, such as silicone, grease or oil to your regulator. Silicone can cause gummy deposits if used inside a regulator improperly. It can also cause the diaphragm or exhaust valves to become slippery, possibly causing them to pop out of their proper position when the diver inhales on the second stage. Lubricants can also cause sand and other foreign particles to build up inside the regulator, leading to internal malfunctions. Any lubricants to be applied to regulator components should be done so only by trained technicians.

Contamination — All internal parts of regulators are made of corrosion resistant materials, such as stainless steel, bronze, or some type of rubber or plastic. Thus, any contamination that causes problems inside the regulator must come from an outside source, such as directly from the scuba tank or from salt or water impurities entering the first stage.

One of the most common sources of contamination leading to regulator malfunction is rust or some other type of contaminant entering the regulator from the scuba tank. It is wise to avoid using your own regulator with tanks that you are unsure of. Also, make sure that your own tanks receive periodic visual inspections in order to insure that they remain free from rust and other contaminants.

Servicing — Every regulator should be serviced by a trained technician at least once a year. If the regulator is used extensively or commercially, it should be serviced every six months, or even more frequently if circumstances dictate. A competent inspection will usually reveal whether or not the regulator is in need of an overhaul or a simple cleaning or tune-up. No amount of washing or careful use can entirely prevent your regulator from becoming out of tune. A simple tune-up will usually involve adjusting the first stage valve to the correct intermediate pressure, along with perhaps a second stage adjustment as well.

WHAT IS AN OVERHAUL?

Anyone performing an overhaul on a regulator should be skilled, competent, and trained in all aspects of regulator repair. He should also be familiar with your particular type of regulator. When turning your regulator in for servicing, let the repairman know the type and amount of use your regulator receives. Are you an instructor, a commercial diver or a "once-a-month" sportdiver? Do you do most of your diving in fresh water, in tropical waters, or beneath frozen layers of ice? For tropical diving, for example, the repairman may want to clean the hoses out to make sure that no bacteria is living inside.

Regulators are designed to be relatively trouble-free, but the more you use them, the more they are exposed to contamination and corrosion. Carbon dust, chlorinated water, hard-water mineral deposits, ozone, rust and salt crystals can cause an accumulation of deposits to gradually build up on the internal parts.

This accumulation may not be readily noticeable, because the process is usually a slow and gradual one. But, if such deposits are allowed to remain in the regulator they can cause hard, crusty, deposits that may interfere with the internal workings of the regulator. This is why it is generally a good idea to have your regulator serviced if it has been in storage for a while or put away for the winter.

Update your Regulator — When turning your regulator in to be serviced, inquire as to whether there is some new equipment or replacement part on the market that might improve your regulator performance. Regulator designs are constantly changing and improving, and many improvements can be incorporated in older models. For example, old

Regulators should be serviced only by qualified repairmen who have the necessary knowledge and tools to accurately diagnose problems, set proper pressures and make any necessary repairs or updates.

neoprene diaphragms and exhaust valves can often be replaced with new, silicone ones. Most manufacturers now stock silicone in place of neoprene parts. Let your repairman know that you wish to *update* your regulator.

Disassembly and Cleaning — An overhaul by a competent repairman will involve disassembly of the entire regulator for routine cleaning and repairing, in the case of corrosion and contamination. When the repairman receives your regulator, he will inspect for any signs of obvious damage, such as bent hoses, dents in the second stage, galls and scratches, or signs of extreme corrosion or misuse. He will make note of the condition in which he received it. *Do not* bring your regulator to the repairman totally *disassembled.* It will only make his job more difficult.

The repairman will then hook the regulator up to an air source to test its operation and check for any signs of malfunctions. This will give him a better idea of what to check for when the regulator is disassembled, if any signs of malfunction are noticeable at this point.

The regulator is then completely disassembled and all parts are cleaned with an ultrasonic cleaner that removes dirt and corrosive deposits. If the regulator is badly corroded, it may be difficult to disassemble and added damage may occur in the process. Ask your repairman to let you know the extent of the damage and what it might cost before he attempts to disassemble it.

All parts will be rinsed and dried thoroughly, then inspected for nicks, and scratches caused by salt crystals or other abrasive deposits. All sealing surfaces are inspected for cracking or flaking of the chrome, and all of the threads will be inspected. All parts which have deteriorated due to age will be replaced, such as O-rings, diaphragms, valve seats or exhaust valves. All deficiencies should be noted on the customer work order, and all damaged parts are usually placed in a bag for the customer to inspect. New parts are installed as soon as the regulator is reassembled.

After reassembly the regulator will be tested for proper operation. Then it will be sent back to the customer. When you receive your regulator from a repairman, test it once or twice before using it to insure that it is operating properly. If you are dissatisifed, return it to the repairman. Often, the valves will take a "seat" after you use the regulator a while, and it may need a little extra adjustment.

Repair Centers — Considering the importance of using a properly operating regulator, the cost of overhauling, retuning or cleaning is extremely reasonable. Most professional dive shops maintain a well-stocked service center for the equipment they sell. Their repair technicians are trained through manufacturer workshops or other training programs. If they are unfamiliar with your particular type of regulator, they can direct you to a reliable place to have it serviced.

In addition to dive shop repair centers, there are various scuba equipment repair centers which specialize in the repair of all types of scuba equipment and accessories. You can mail your regulator to them along with any special instructions, and have it serviced and returned in a relatively short amount of time. Or, you may send your regulator back to the factory where it can be overhauled by specially trained personnel.

BASIC TROUBLESHOOTING

By keeping your eyes and ear attuned to your regulator, you can spot most trouble before it becomes serious. Some of the common symptoms of trouble discussed in this section will give you a good idea of how to locate the potential source of malfunction or contamination before it has a chance to destroy your regulator or cause even more serious problems while you're diving. However, corrective action that involves *disassembly* of your regulator should be performed by a qualified regulator repairman.

Inspect the Sintered Filter — The small air filter located on the first stage of the regulator is called the sintered filter. Any contamination or foreign matter entering the regulator from the tank will usually show up on this filter. Tiny particles and chemicals can pass through this filter directly into your regulator, so it is imperative to protect this filter with a dust cap when the regulator is not in use. Check the sintered filter from time to time for any of the following:

1. *A Reddish-Brown Discoloration* — If the sintered filter reveals reddish-brown specks on its surface, the most probable cause is rust from the scuba tank. Rust particles from the tank will clog the pores of the filter screen, and can also work their way to the interior of the regulator. Rust

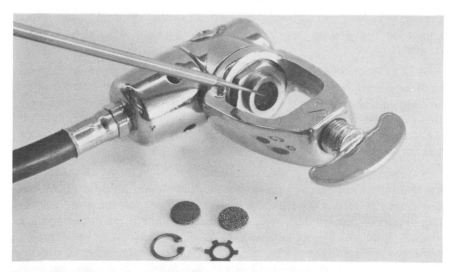

The sintered filter is the tiny air filter located at the inlet to the first stage of the regulator assembly. It should be examined frequently for signs of corrosion or contamination that may indicate damage in the interior of the regulator. Whenever the regulator is not in use, this filter should always be covered with a protective dust cap.

particles can dig into O-rings, can pit the air valves and lodge themselves into close tolerance areas, causing parts to wear.

Rust from the tank is one of the most common culprits of regulator malfunctions. Using rental tanks and other people's tanks that you are unfamiliar with can very easily lead to this problem.

2. *Black Particles* — If black particles show up on the sintered filter, these are a good indication of carbon dust entering the regulator as a result of a faulty air compressor. The black particles are the activated charcoal that has not been filtered out of the air compressor properly when filling the tank. Carbon particles inside the tank will resemble a black, dry powder, and can enter the regulator through the first stage sintered filter.

3. *Turquoise, Greenish, Or Chalky White Coating* — If the sintered filter takes on any of these colors, it is a good indication that salt water has entered the inlet of the first stage. Salt can cause damage and corrosion inside the regulator. Chalky white specks around the filter are usually dried salt crystals, which take on a turquoise or greenish appearance when they have had time to react with the brass or bronze filter material. Salt water can carry in marine organisms and other abrasive matter that can damage the regulator.

Note: Some of the newer regulators now have stainless steel sintered filters. Stainless steel will not exhibit any color change when exposed to salt water, (as do the bronze and brass sintered filters). If your regulator has a stainless steel sintered filter, you will want to be extra careful not to allow salt water to enter the high pressure inlet, since interior corrosion will not be evident externally.

4. *Tiny Paint-like Flakes* — If tiny flakes resembling pieces of chipped paint are found on the sintered filter, they could be particles of lining that have come loose from the interior of the tank. The color of these particles will depend upon the color of the lining inside your tank. Not all tanks have an interior lining, but this can often be a problem with those types that do.

Corrective Action: If the sintered filter reveals any of the above discolorations, the source of the contamination should be determined. In many cases, the tank will have to be given a visual inspection, and the tank valve should be inspected as well. The regulator should be inspected by a trained technician who will be able to determine the extent of the damage. The proper corrective action can vary from a simple replacement of the sintered filter to a complete overhaul of the regulator. The longer you wait before taking corrective action, the greater the extent of damage that may occur inside your regulator.

Free-Flowing Regulator — A hissing noise coming from the second stage will usually indicate that the regulator is free flowing. This can indicate improper internal adjustments or damaged internal parts. Foreign particles which enter the first stage (dust, dirt, sand, salt, etc.) can interfere with the functioning of the high pressure valve seat in the first stage, causing improper internal air pressures. Free flowing can also be caused by a purge button that is stuck open or has foreign matter obstructing its operation.

Contamination in the second stage can also cause the regulator to free flow. If this happens underwater, the free flow can often be alleviated by simply removing the regulator from your mouth and shaking the second stage or depressing the purge button to dislodge any contaminants. If this does not immediately alleviate the free flow, return to the surface and do not use the regulator until it has been repaired.

Regulators with a pilot valve in the second stage assembly are very sensitive to changes in pressure, due to inherent features designed to reduce inhalation effort and improve the performance of the regulator. The sensitivity of the valve, however, can cause the regulator to free flow or to deliver excess air under the right conditions. For example, slight pressure changes caused by surge and swells in shallow water or currents may precipitate this. If your regulator has a pilot valve in the second stage, be aware of this and always read the manufacturer's instructions prior to use.

Hard Inhalation — Excessive resistance to inhalation can be caused by any of the following: 1) Low tank air pressure 2) A clogged or plugged sintered filter. 3) Improper internal pressures within the regulator, which indicates damaged or improperly operating internal components. Salt water corrosion is a common cause of hard breathing. Internal parts become encrusted with salt crystals, causing them to stick or operate sluggishly.

Hard Exhalation — Difficulty in exhalation through a regulator may be caused by: 1) The exhaust valve may be stuck to its seating surface. 2) An obstruction exists within the exhaust chamber of the regulator. Normal aging, exposure to ozone, and the introduction of chlorine into the second stage can cause the internal rubber parts (exhaust valves and diaphragms) to become dry and brittle, and to deteriorate or crack.

Water Entering Second Stage During Inhalation — If water enters the second stage of the regulator when inhaling, the probable causes may be one of the following: 1) A torn or deteriorated mouthpiece. 2) The second stage clamp retaining ring may be loose. 3) Deterioration of the second stage exhalation valve, or an improperly seated or torn exhaust valve. 4) The diaphragm may be torn, damaged or improperly seated in the second stage. If water leakage is allowed to persist in the second stage, it can lead to a complete flooding of the second stage.

Air Leakage Around the First Stage — If air is found to be leaking from the first stage water inlet holes, internal damage should be suspected and major repairs may be in order. If leaking is noticed around the high and low pressure hose attachments, this can often be traced to damaged O-rings on the fitting or on the port plug. If air leakage is noticed from the hoses themselves, the entire hose assembly should be replaced.

Erratic Air Flow — An erratic air flow can be caused by a second stage which is not properly tuned. If may also indicate that internal parts are sticking, or otherwise functioning improperly. An incorrect intermediate stage pressure can also produce an erratic air flow.

Since the second stage fills with water anytime you remove your mouthpiece while underwater, this exposure to salt water or hard mineral water can eventually effect its performance, particularly if foreign matter is not properly rinsed from the second stage. If an erratic air flow is noticed, it may be time to take your regulator in for an inspection and tune-up.

REGULATOR ACCESSORIES

Anytime accessories are added to the first stage of the regulator, such as gauges, inflators for the BC, or octopus second stages, always make sure they are attached to the correct pressure port. Usually, only the submersible pressure gauge connects to the high pressure outlet. Most other accessories will attach to the low pressure ports.

Octopus Second Stage — An aid to safe diving that is appearing on an increasing number of regulator systems is the octopus second stage. If you wish to add an octopus second stage to your own regulator assembly, it is recommended that you use a second stage with an operating pressure compatible to your own regulator's intermediate pressure. Using a matching second stage will fill this requirement.

When attaching a second stage octopus assembly, make sure it is connected to a low pressure port. To protect the regulator from damage, secure it close to the diver's body with some type of quick disconnect retaining strap, where it can also be easily reached in an emergency.

A recent innovation in octopus designs incorporates a second stage as an integral part of the inflator mechanism. It is easily attached to a buoyancy compensating unit in the same manner that most power inflators are installed.

High Pressure Valve Adaptor — Many European valves, tanks and regulators are designed to withstand pressures as high as 5,000 or 6,000 psi. A special fitting called a DIN connection (DIN = German Industrial Standard) that is specifically designed to accommodate higher pressures is used with this type of European tank and regulator.

If you plan on using your U.S. made regulator on a European tank valve, there is a DIN valve adaptor available for this purpose, but you must insure that the tank pressure does not exceed the maximum safe operating pressure of your regulator. Some regulators can be modified to accept DIN connectors, and some types have DIN connectors available from the manufacturers, who produce them for their European market. Always check with the manufacturer for specifications pertaining to the DIN connection.

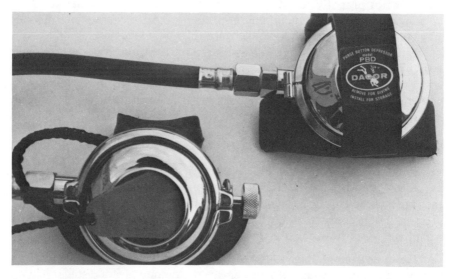

Some manufacturers supply a spacing wedge or device with their regulator assemblies. This device relieves pressure on the second stage valve seat by depressing the purge button when the regulator is not in use.

Buoyancy Compensators And Inflators

Buoyancy compensators (also referred to as BC s) provide the diver with the means to have direct control of his buoyancy at the surface or underwater. They are personal flotation devices that can be used for swimming or resting on the surface, or for adjusting a diver's buoyancy underwater. When used underwater buoyancy compensators allow the diver to compensate for wetsuit compression resulting from increased pressure at depths. BC s also allow the diver to maintain neutral buoyancy underwater, regardless of depth or activity, and provide the added "lift" that may be needed for carrying heavy camera equipment, or a goodie bag filled with game or artifacts.

There is a wide variety of different types of BC s currently on the market, available in an assortment of popular colors and choice of accessories. Buoyancy compensators incorporate the same basic principles and functions, but differences in design cater to individual diving needs and preferences. The buoyancy compensator is an important part of the diver's underwater life support system, and it should be properly maintained to function dependably in its intended capacity.

TYPES OF BC S

Inflatable Vests — The inflatable vest, designed for use on the surface only, may be considered the "forerunner" of the modern buoyancy compensator. It is primarily a swim vest, giving the snorkeler or swimmer an added means of flotation in an emergency situation. It utilizes a CO_2 cartridge detonator for quick inflation, and is also equipped with a simple oral inflation device. The vest encircles the swimmer's neck and shoulders, providing support to float the swimmer or snorkeler's head above the surface of the water. Some inflatable vests do come equipped with over-pressure relief valves for use underwater.

Horse Collar BC s — The horse collar BC, similar in appearance to the inflatable swim vest is aptly named for the design evolving from the early survival vests used by the military. This design has been the "workhorse" of the diving industry throughout the years. Today's horse collar style of buoyancy compensator is actually an enlarged and more complex version of the earlier survival vest, incorporating additional features designed to enhance the diver's underwater capabilities and comfort.

Horse collar style BC s are equipped with over-pressure relief valves which prevent the vest from rupturing when the bag is filled to capacity through a specially designed spring that allows air to be vented from the bag when the internal air pressure has reached a pre-determined pressure. CO^2 cartridge detonators are usually installed in most horse collar BC s, allowing for instant inflation in an emergency. A flexible corrugated hose with a special mouthpiece provides a means of orally inflating the BC. Power inflators can also be easily installed if the manufacturer has not already done so.

Horse collar BC's are very popular due to their compactness, ease of operation, and relatively simple maintenance. They are usually the least expensive type of buoyancy compensator available and currently offer the largest variety of designs, styles, colors and sizes. Horse collar buoyancy compensators can be used for both scuba diving and snorkeling activities, as they support the diver's head well above the surface of the water when fully inflated.

Back Mounted BC's — Back mounted BC's, first introduced into the diving industry in 1970, represent a radical departure from the traditional design of personal flotation and buoyancy compensating devices. Back mounted BC's feature an inflatable horseshoe-shaped bag that is mounted to the diver's backpack and conforms to the outside perimeters of the scuba tank. Its function and operation is similiar to the horse collar style of buoyancy compensators, but it is carried on the diver's back, rather than around his neck and chest area.

There are two types of back mounted BC's — the hard shell and the soft pack type. The hard shell type features a hard plastic or fiberglass shell mounted around the air bladder, to streamline and protect the bladder. The soft packs are fabricated with essentially the same material as horse collar BC's. Back pack mounted BC's may vary in design from a simple buoyancy compensator mounted to the backpack to the incorporation of an entire diving system (weight belt, tank, regulator, inflation device and backpack) in a single unit. With the latter design, a diver could remove his entire diving system with the release of a single strap.

Most back mounted BC's do not have CO^2 cartridge assemblies, or separate compressed air "emergency" fill bottles. However, they usually contain both oral and power inflation devices, as well as over-pressure relief valves. They are not designed to be used for snorkeling, since they can not be used when removed from the backpack and may even be semi-

Buoyancy compensator units are currently manufactured in four basic styles: the inflatable vest, the horse collar BC, the back mounted unit and the jacket type BC.

permanently attached to the backpack. Their flotation design utilizes a high center of buoyancy and low center of gravity, providing most of the lift at the top of the back for comfortable underwater swimming.

Jacket Type BC's — The jacket type BC is the most recent innovation in the design of boyancy compensators, and is steadily gaining in popularity among divers. The jacket type BC provides flotation in both the back and front chest area of the diver, and is easy to slip in and out of with its wrap around jacket-like design. Provisions for attaching the tank may also be incorporated within the design of the BC, or a backpack may be used in conjunction with the jacket BC, depending on the manufacturer.

The jacket type BC supports the full weight of the tank, but spreads the weight of the tank over a wide surface area across the shoulders. This effectively distributes the weight more comfortably than do ordinary tank shoulder straps. The jacket type BC provides lift at the shoulders, where it is needed on the surface, and also provides lift at the top of the back, where it is most comfortable for underwater swimming.

CONSTRUCTION

All professional quality buoyancy compensators available through dive shops incorporate over pressure relief valves, regardless of the style or model of the BC. They may offer oral or power inflation devices, or both, as a normal means of inflating the BC, and may or may not have CO_2 cartridge detonators installed for emergency quick inflation purposes. Some models offer power deflator devices and quick dump valves as an additional means of deflating the vest. Most BC's are displayed without the power inflation device installed, but this can be easily purchased and installed at the dive shop.

Single Bag Construction — BC's that utilize a single bag construction are generally fabricated from a heavy strength nylon material, coated on one side with neoprene rubber which is adhesively bonded to the material. After the BC is cut to the desired shape, the seams are taped both inside and out with a strong adhesive. This creates an exceptionally strong construction, but may be difficult to repair should the bag become punctured or otherwise damaged.

Double Bag Construction — Buoyancy compensators that are designed with a double bag construction feature an inner air bladder of strong polyurethane plastic. The seams are normally sealed together using an electronic fusing process similar to a microwave oven. The unique construction method employed in this process allows for an optimum type material for internal air retention, and an outer structural shell designed for high stress and abrasion. Grommets installed at various points in the outer bag allow for the venting of air or water from the confined space between the two bags.

PATCHING YOUR BUOYANCY COMPENSATOR

Buoyancy compensators are extremely difficult to puncture, due to the exceptional strength of the materials used in their construction. However, in the event that something should cause a tear or puncture in the fabric of the BC, most can be repaired and restored to their original operating condition.

If the material in your buoyancy compensator needs patching, you may return the BC to the manufacturer for the necessary repairs, or you can obtain the manufacturer recommended repair kit designed to be used for your particular BC. Once you have obtained the proper repair kit, patch the BC according to the instructions enclosed, always using the material and adhesives supplied in the patching kit.

Due to the wide variety of materials used in the construction of buoyancy compensators, it is usually not advisable to attempt to repair the vest with anything but the BC repair kit recommended by the manufacturer. However, small punctures or tears on either single bag BCs or on the internal bags in BCs can be effectively repaired in the field with most adhesive systems (contact adhesives, water bed adhesives and epoxy systems) by using any rubberized material or plastic-coated material that is compatible.

Test the compatibility of the patching material with a small "test" piece first to insure that it bonds effectively.

Do not attempt to repair the BC within an inch of any of the seams, or around the high stress areas immediately below the neck (on horse-collar BCs) or within an inch of accessory protruberances. Field repairs are designed for "emergency" short term exposure, and the vest should always be returned to the manufacturer for final inspection. Always keep in mind that unauthorized repairs on the BC could jeopardize the integrity of the BC, and could also void the manufacturer's warrantee.

Patching Procedure — For small cuts, holes or tears in the inner bladder of the BC, a typical repair procedure recommended by most manufacturers includes the following steps. Always use the material and adhesives supplied by the manufacturer. (*Caution:* The diver could experience a catastrophic failure with the vest if repaired incorrectly around stress areas.)

1. Locate the puncture or tear in the inner bladder by visually inspecting the surface. With a ballpoint pen, mark the location of the puncture or tear. If the source of the leak cannot be located visually, then install all of the BC accessories on the inner bladder only and inflate the inner bladder assembly. Immerse in water and search for signs of escaping bubbles that may indicate a leak. Mark the area with a pen.

2. After marking the punctured area, use the patching material supplied by the manufacturer to cut a patch of the corresponding size and shape desired. Leave at least a 1/2" to 3/4" margin which allows the patch to overlap the hole, so it will adhere strongly around all sides of the hole.

3. If the puncture or tear in the bladder exhibits ragged edges, trim the edges with a pair of sharp scissors. Then roughen the area around the hole and one side of the patch with a fine piece of sandpaper (#320 garnet is most commonly used). Most adhesives will not adhere to a smooth surface strong enough to form a good bond.

4. Clean the area around the hole and the patch with rubbing alcohol, allowing the alcohol to evaporate throughly before preparing the adhesive. Make sure the patch and the area surrounding the hole are dry and completely free of foreign matter, such as particles left by the sandpaper.

5. Prepare the adhesive, following the instructions issued by the manufacturer. Apply a small amount of adhesive onto the roughened surface of the patch that will come in contact with the outside skin of the bladder. Do not apply adhesive to any portion of the patch that will not make contact with the outer bladder skin, as it will stick to the opposite inner side of the bladder. Before patching the hole, allow the adhesive to set according to the amount of time recommended (this is usually from 30 to 60 minutes).

6. Position the patch over the hole by applying a constant and firm

pressure. Let set approximately 24 hours (or as otherwise recommended). Place a flat, weighted object on top of the patch while it is curing to insure an effective bond. After the patching procedure has been completed, test the integrity of the patch by submerging the inflated bladder in water while inspecting for signs of leakage.

CO_2 CARTRIDGES AND DETONATORS

CO_2 (carbon dioxide) detonating systems are installed on buoyancy compensators to provide a rapid method of inflating the BC for buoyancy purposes. The CO_2 device is designed for self-contained rapid inflation, and can be of significant benefit in any number of diving situations.

Maintenance Procedures —

1. Remove the CO_2 cartridge and visually inspect the detonator, to insure that the pin extends and retracts when the nylon lanyard is pulled.

Caution: Make sure the lanyard is in its "up" or "armed" position before screwing the CO_2 cartridge into the detonator. When reinstalling the cartridge, lightly pull the lanyard down to make sure that the pin does touch the CO_2 cartridge within a 20° arc. Do not exert enough force to cause the cartridge to detonate or to cause an indentation in the cartridge.

2. Some of the older types of detonators utilize schroeder valves, similar to the small valves within the valve stem on a tire. After prolonged use or storage, these valves may become clogged or frozen.

All manufacturers now recommend that these types of valves be removed permanently from the detonator mounting stud. Schroeder valves were originally installed to prevent water from entering the detonator from the vest and causing corrosion. However, with the frequency that CO_2 cartridges are changed and the practice of good maintenance techniques, they are no longer installed in the detonators in BCs.

3. Flush the buoyancy compensator or inflatable vest out with fresh water when the cartridges are removed, to make sure that the detonators are not clogged. A good rinse that includes forcing the water through the detonator mechanisms should remove any particles or pieces of sand that may be clogging the detonator.

Periodically lubricate the metal insert inside the detonator. With the cartridges removed, spray a light coat of WD-40, or apply a small amount of vaseline or silicone to the inside of the detonator. Then cautiously open the tank valve and direct a low pressure stream of air into the detonator. This will distribute the lubricant and will also blow away any residual moisture or foreign matter.

4. It is a good idea to check the firing mechanism by detonating a CO_2 cartridge at least once a year in your BC to make sure the vest inflates properly. If the cartridge is due for a change because of rust, this is a good

DETONATOR ASSEMBLIES

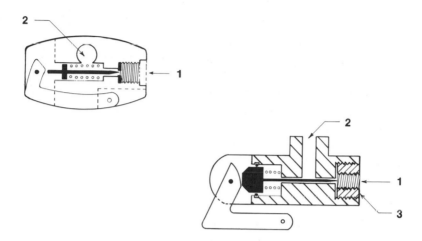

1. CO2 Cartridge Mount 2. Vest Stud Mount 3. Adaptor Insert.

time to conduct the test by firing the old cartridge. Always replace the cartridge after testing with a new one.

Damged Threads in the Detonator — The entire detonator should be replaced if the threads become stripped or worn excessively. In some recently designed BC's, the CO_2 cartridge screws into an adaptor which can also be removed from the detonator mechanism if the cartridge becomes frozen or the threads become damaged. The CO_2 cartridge and the adaptor can be removed together and the entire detonator assembly will remain in place. Thus, only a new adaptor will need to be purchased and installed, instead of the entire detonator mechanism.

To Remove and Install Cartridges — Whenever the CO_2 cartridge is being removed from the detonator, hold the detonator firmly with a pair of pliers. NOTE: The pliers should have a soft cloth in their jaws to prevent galling of the plastic. Never hold the BC material itself to remove the cartridge, as the detonator assembly could be pulled apart from the vest.

Whenever installing CO_2 cartridges, apply a light coat of silicone grease or vaseline to the threads of the cartridge. Do not apply too liberally, as the air ports could become clogged or could collect foreign particles, causing the detonator to malfunction.

When reinstalling the cartridges, do not overtighten. Excessive force can cause the detonator to crack. Also, be careful not to damage the threads by cross threading the cartridge.

ABOUT ORAL INFLATORS

Oral inflator mechanisms provide a means of inflating and deflating the vest or BC by depressing a button on a specially designed mouthpiece and exhaling into the vest. The exhaled air is transferred into the vest through a long hose, and is sealed in the vest upon release of the button. The vest is deflated by holding the valve higher than the air level in the BC and depressing the button. This will allow the air to exit from the bag and it will deflate, thus decreasing the diver's buoyancy.

To Remove and Install Inflators — Inflator mechanisms can be easily removed and installed on their properly designed hoses, always taking care not to damage the inflator mechanism through improper handling.

1. To remove the inflator mechanism from the hose assembly, first remove the inflator hose retaining clamp, or tyrap, from the spot at which the hose attaches to the inflator.

2. Carefully insert a small screwdriver underneath the end of the hose at the point where the hose slips over the inflator valve.

3. Cautiously move the screwdriver around the circumference of the inflator valve body until the hose is separated from the inflator. Remove the inflator mechanism from the hose.

Caution: Do not lift the screwdriver up in a prying manner, as this always results in a torn hose. Just wriggle the screwdriver back and forth very gently until the hose separates from the inflator.

4. Before installing the inflator back on the hose, roughen the inside of the hose with a light grit sandpaper. Then clean thoroughly, using rubbing alcohol and a lint-free cloth.

To install the oral inflator back on the hose, first apply a light coat of neoprene cement inside of the opening on the inflator hose. Apply an even coat that extends about one inch inside the opening.

5. Apply another coat of neoprene cement on the outside of the corresponding end of the inflator mechanism to be installed on the hose.

6. Let dry approximately five to ten minutes. Then apply a second very thin coat of neoprene cement to just the end of the inflator mechanism (as described in step 5), but not to the inflator hose.

7. While the second coat is still wet, insert the inflator mechanism into the end of the inflator hose, positioning the inflator mouthpiece facing upwards toward the mouth, where it is comfortable to use in the water.

8. Install the appropriate retaining clamp or tyrap, and allow the wetsuit cement to dry thoroughly before using the inflator.

Troubleshooting Oral Inflators — Due to a minimum of parts and simplicity of design, oral inflators are relatively trouble free devices. Mal-

INSTALLING INFLATORS

1. Remove the old retaining ring or tyrap.

2. Use a screwdriver to separate the hose from the inflator.

3. Apply neoprene cement to the end of the inflator and corresponding hose end.

4. Install the inflator on the hose and secure with a tyrap or retaining ring.

ORAL INFLATORS

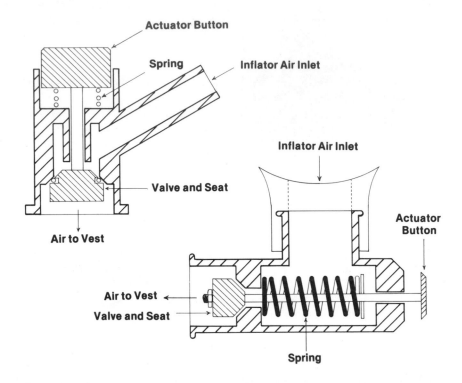

functions are also often very simple to locate and usually involve minimal repairs. However, when in doubt about the safe operation or proper assemblage of any part of your BC, always consult a qualified repairman or return it to the manufacturer for repairs.

1. If the inflator button sticks in upon depressing it, and then pops out when you pull on it, this may be caused by contamination of the valve stem at the point at which it enters the housing of the valve. This may be corrected by actuating the valve a number of times in water in order to rinse out the contaminating particles.

2. If the oral inflator actuating button flops back and forth, you may suspect a broken spring or valve assembly, or may suspect that the assembly has simply come apart or become "disassembled". If this happens, the oral inflator mechanism must be taken off the BC, and further inspected to locate the source of the malfunction.

In some older designs, a cir-clip which is used at the base of the cone spring may have become loosened and fallen off. This condition manifests itself by an apparent lack of spring action upon depressing the stem. It can not be repaired, and replacement of the entire valve assembly is necessary.

3. If bubbles are noticed exiting from the inflator mouthpiece, this may be caused by improper seating or contamination of the valve. The inflator should be flushed out with water while depressing the valve and directing the flow of water into the vest. Squeeze the water back out of the BC while depressing the valve.

Occasionally, when a mouthpiece is leaking, it can be traced to foreign objects in the valve seat. If the leakage continues even after removal of the foreign object, this may be the result of permanent deformations left in the rubber. Often, the resultant leak can be stopped by depressing the button and turning the stem in a clockwise direction a half a turn or more. However, if the bubbles persist, the valve will have to be taken off the vest and further disassembled to locate the malfunction.

ABOUT POWER INFLATORS

Power inflators are designed to use the low pressure air tapped off of the low pressure port from the first stage of the regulator to inflate the vest. This eliminates the need to remove the regulator from the mouth to fill the vest. Instead, the vest can be quickly filled with compressed air from the scuba tank by actuating a button or lever. This allows for greater ease of movement underwater with accessory items such as camera equipment, as well as added ease in adjusting the diver's buoyancy, regardless of depth or activity.

An additional benefit of using a power inflator on a buoyancy compensator is that, in most cases, the low pressure hose can be quick-released from the device and a variety of pneumatic tools (both in, under and out of the water) can be employed by the diver. This would include, for example, such tools as those used for filling tires or lift bags.

Installation — Power inflators are installed on the BC in the same manner as oral inflators. However, extreme caution should be exercised during the initial installation of the power inflator assembly to the regulator first stage. If the power inflator is inadvertently attached to the high pressure port in the first stage, when the tank air is turned on the low pressure hose will burst, or the entire low pressure inflation device may explode.

Always attach the inflator hose to the low pressure port (often marked "LP") of the first stage. If, on a new installation you are not sure as to which is the high pressure or low pressure port, first conduct a test with a submersible pressure gauge to determine the proper port.

You will need a full tank of air to conduct the test. Attach the first stage of the regulator to the tank valve. Then attach the submersible pressure gauge to either of the ports in question. Turn the air on slowly, with the face of the gauge facing away from you. Examine the reading on the gauge. If the reading indicates a full tank of air (somewhere between 2,000 and 3,000 psi), this is the high pressure port. If the reading indicates a low pressure (somewhere between 100 and 140 psi), then this is the low pressure port.

How Power Inflators Work — The low pressure air is supplied to the inflator valve assembly by a low pressure quick disconnect hose coming off the first stage of the regulator. Upon actuation of the inflator valve, by depressing the inflator button or lever, the air is passed from the tank through the first stage of the regulator out one of the low pressure orifices through the quick disconnect hose and then to the power inflator. The air will pass through the valve and go directly into the BC, thus inflating the BC.

Some power inflators allow you to deflate the vest in the same way as the oral inflator, by holding it above the level of the air in the BC and depressing the button, allowing the air to escape. On some types of BC's you must use a separate hose with the oral inflator mouthpiece on it to deflate the vest, or you may deflate the vest through a special quick dump valve or through a power deflator, if your BC incorporates these features.

A recent innovation in power inflator design incorporates a second stage designed to be used as an octopus regulator. The regulator assembly housed in the power inflator mechanism uses low pressure air provided for the power inflator as an emergency supply of air for the diver.

Maintenance of Power Inflators — The power inflator is a sophisticated mechanism. Always take care to protect the quick disconnect end of the hose and the power inflator from contact with dirt, sand or other foreign particles that may accumulate and destroy the O-rings or cause leakage or malfunctions.

1. After every dive, flush and rinse with fresh waster by directing the stream of water into the inflator. Flush out with water and activate all controls and moving parts, checking for freedom and ease of operation.

2. Never squirt or spray any type of silicone or oil lubricants into an inflator, as this will cause foreign particles to accumulate, producing possible malfunctions.

3. If air leaks around the quick disconnect fitting on the hose when attached to the power inflator, this may be caused by a damaged O-ring inside the quick disconnect fitting. If this is the cause, the O-ring should be replaced with the proper size O-ring. You may also suspect a nick or gouge in the quick disconnect O-ring seat on the power inflator, so this should also be given a visual inspection.

4. If the vest keeps inflating, and the button is stuck to the down position, this may be caused by dirt or foreign particles around the stem of the inflator button. Inspect this area, giving it a thorough rinsing before inflating the BC again.

5. If the vest keeps inflating after the inflator button is released and the

POWER INFLATOR ASSEMBLIES

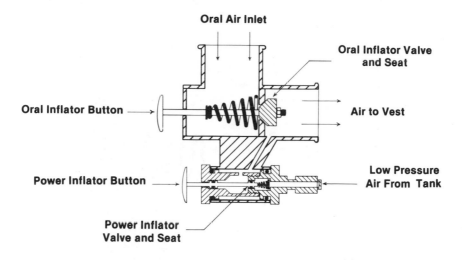

Oral Air Inlet

Oral Inflator Valve and Seat

Oral Inflator Button

Air to Vest

Power Inflator Button

Low Pressure Air From Tank

Power Inflator Valve and Seat

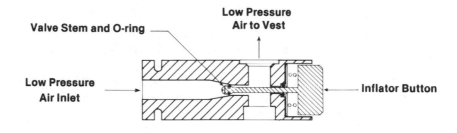

Valve Stem and O-ring

Low Pressure Air to Vest

Low Pressure Air Inlet

Inflator Button

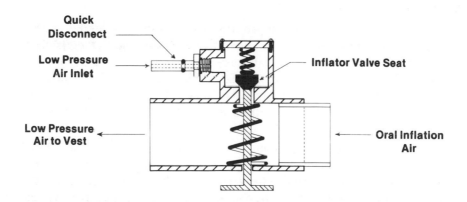

Quick Disconnect

Low Pressure Air Inlet

Inflator Valve Seat

Low Pressure Air to Vest

Oral Inflation Air

OVER PRESSURE RELIEF VALVE ASSEMBLY

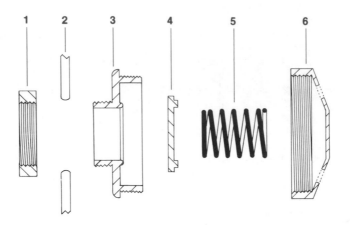

1. Retaining Nut 2. Vest Bladder 3. Relief Valve Body 4. Valve 5. Spring 6. Vent Cap.

button returns to its normal position, then you may suspect either a damaged valve or valve seat, or contamination inside the power inflator. Any time the power inflator sticks while diving and passes air to the vest unintended, it should be disconnected immediately and not used again until the source of the malfunction has been discovered and corrected.

If major problems are suspected or repairs are required, always send it to a qualified repairman or back to the manufacturer before using it again. Don't jeopardize the integrity or the warrantee on your BC by attempting to perform major repairs yourself.

CHECKING FOR LEAKS IN THE BUOYANCY COMPENSATOR.

To inspect the buoyancy compensator for leaks in the material, in the seams or in any of the accessory mechanisms, make sure the CO_2 cartridges are installed in the detonator mechanisms prior to testing. If the BC utilizes a power inflator, the low pressure hose should be attached and pressurized. Fully inflate the BC, and immerse the BC in a large tub of water. Inspect the following areas for signs of escaping air bubbles, which may indicate possible leakage:

1. Inspect the BC bag assembly — In double bag construction, some residual air will leak out of the drain grommets on the BC's outer bag, to vent the air that has been trapped between the two bags. If air continues to escape, then the outer bag should be partially removed to inspect for leaking

areas in the inner bag assembly. In BC's of single bag construction, inspect all seams carefully.

2. Inspect accessories — Inspect all areas where accessories are sealed and mounted to the bag. If leaks are detected around the mountings, inspect thoroughly for cracks. Often a simple tightening will stop the leakage, if there are no visual signs of damage.

3. Inspect the oral inflator inlet and the area where it attaches to the hose. If any leakage is coming out of the oral inflator inlet, usually a simple rinsing with fresh water will stop the leakage, unless physical damage is evident.

4. Inspect the power inflator — Check the point at which the low pressure hose quick disconnect fitting attaches to the inflator for any signs of air bubbles. Listen to the power inflator assembly for any unusual sounds that may indicate internal problems. If leakage is detected in the power inflator, do not use it again until the problem has been remedied, as the BC could fully inflate if the valve opens all of a sudden.

5. Actuate the power inflator valve to check for proper sealing and freedom of movement. If any sticking of the valve is noticed, do not use the inflator until the valve has been disassembled and repaired by a competent repairman.

6. Over pressure relief valves — Inspect around the exhaust holes for signs of leakage. If none is detected, squeeze the vest to check for proper valve operation. If the over pressure relief valve is not functioning, do not use the BC.

7. CO_2 Detonators — Inspect the points at which the detonator mechanism is attached to the vest for any signs of leakage. Also inspect for leakage around the CO_2 cartridges where they enter the detonator mechanism.

CARE AND CLEANING OF THE BC

Wash the buoyancy compensator after each dive, flushing water both inside and out, and between the inner and outer bags. Direct a stream of water into the mouth piece of the oral inflator valve, and drain the water back through the mouth piece. If your BC so allows, remove the over pressure relief valve assembly and rinse all components.

To drain the water from the BC, reinstall the over pressure relief valve, and orally inflate the vest. Turn the vest upside down so that the drain hose is at the lowest point. Depress the inflator button and squeeze the vest. The sudden rush of air should force the remaining water to exit from the interior of the vest through the inflator hose.

A commercial BC conditioner may be used in the final rinse, to inhibit the growth of mold or mildew, and to keep the BC fresh and odor-free. The best way to prevent the growth of harmful molds and bacteria is to use the buoyancy compensator frequently in salt water. Salt water effectively inhibits the growth of fungus and molds, and most of the materials used in the BC (with the exception of some detonating mechanisms) are impervious to salt water, but can be damaged by fresh water fungus and chlorines.

Buoyancy compensators should be stored partially inflated. For prolonged storage, a small amount of silicone lubricant may be applied to the rubber parts of the BC, but *do not spray* silicone inside the bag itself or on to the oral or power inflator mouthpiece assemblies. Store the buoyancy compensator with the hose on the downward side, so that residual moisture drains to the hose assembly. Then, after a day or two, depress the inflator button to allow the residual water to drain from the buoyancy compensator.

ABOUT THE A.I.R. II

The A.I.R. II *(Alternate Inflator Regulator),* introduced by Scubapro in 1979, is a combination backup regulator and power inflator mechanism.

The A.I.R. II should be checked for proper functioning before each dive. With the quick-disconnect removed and the unit unpressurized, check the A.I.R. II for leaks by placing the mouthpiece in your mouth while plugging the quick-disconnect inlet. Attempt to inhale applying moderate pressure. There should be no air escaping through the unit. Now exhale, to check for proper functioning of the exhaust valve.

Next, attach pressurized hose to A.I.R. II and listen at the quick-disconnect for any audible air leaks. Then inhale and exhale on the mouthpiece to insure proper operation. Activate the power inflator mechanism to check for any air leakage, auto inflation or other malfunctions. Minor contaminants lodged in the mechanism can often be dislodged by disconnecting and reconnecting the A.I.R. II while holding it submerged in water. Any repairs should be done only by the manufacturer or an authorized service center.

Due to the corrosion-resistant materials inherent in its construction, the unit is relatively maintenance free, and should be maintained in the same manner that you maintain your regulator and B.C. power inflator. Basic maintenance includes a thorough fresh water rinse after diving. In addition you can disconnect and reconnect the unit to its low pressure air supply hose while it is submerged in fresh water. This will flush out the inner mechanisms with fresh water to prevent salt crystals from building up inside. Then take the unit out of water and activate the purge button and the power inflator to insure that all of the moisture is flushed from the mechanism. Caution: Never connect the unit to its low pressure inflator hose when the hose is non pressurized if there is salt water in it, as the salt water can flow back into the first stage of the regulator, causing possible damage.

Underwater Gauges

Routine maintenance for underwater gauges includes a fresh water rinse after every dive, paying attention to any openings or features unique to your particular type of gauge. Extreme heat, prolonged exposure to sunlight, and rough handling and treatment can harm the fine instrumentation of most gauges. Anytime the calibration or operation of a gauge is in question, return it to your local dealer or manufacturer for adjustment and repairs.

DEPTH GAUGES

Depth gauges are relatively trouble-free pieces of equipment, but proper maintenance is necessary to insure accuracy and reliability. There are several different designs of depth gauges manufactured today from which the diver can choose.

Capillary Depth Gauge — The simplest and least expensive type of depth gauge on the market today is the capillary depth gauge. This gauge consists of a small plastic tube that opens on one end and is mounted around the perimeter of a calibrated dial. Water enters the tube at its open end, compressing the air as the diver descends. The calibration on the dial that corresponds to the thin line separating the water from the air inside the tube indicates the correct depth.

Capillary depth gauges are most accurate up to depths of about eighty feet. At depths beyond this, the graduation of the scale on the gauge becomes very close, causing difficulty in reading the exact depth indicated. Before the dive, always check to insure that no water has remained in the tube from the previous dive, as this will cause an error in the reading. This type of gauge is susceptible to damage or inaccuracies when beach diving through heavy surf, churned up sand or turbid muddy waters, due to the ease with which foreign matter may enter the tube in the gauge.

The capillary depth gauge is very easy to maintain, due to its simple design and lack of moving parts. To thoroughly rinse the gauge, remove the clear plastic tube from its calibrated setting, remove the caps from the end of the tube, and flush the tube with fresh water. The interior can be further cleaned, if necessary, with a pipe cleaner or small brush. When reassembling the gauge, reinstall the tube in its correct position, since the gauge could register erroneously if the tube is installed backwards.

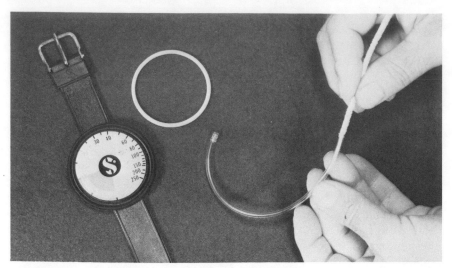

Sand and foreign particles can contaminate the plastic tube in a capillary depth gauge and effect the accuracy of the reading. For a thorough cleaning, disassemble the gauge, rinse all parts in fresh water, and use a pipe cleaner or small brush to clean the interior of the tube.

Oil Filled Depth Gauges — An oil filled depth gauge is composed of a pressure sensitive mechanism immersed in an oil-filled housing. The reading on this type of gauge is almost instantaneous with the change in pressure, due to the non-compressibility of the oil within the casing. Oil-filled gauges are less susceptible to damage from shock or rough use than most other types of gauges, due to the entire mechanism being encased in the surrounding oil. Normally, the case itself must be damaged before the mechanism will fail to operate correctly.

Due to the fact that oil-filled gauges are completely enclosed mechanisms, they are relatively trouble-free instruments, as contaminants can not enter the interior. They require a minimum of maintenance, which amounts to a simple rinsing with fresh water after the dive.

Bourdon Tube Depth Gauges — Most depth gauges used by sport-divers employ a Bourdon tube to sense the change in pressure underwater. This in turn causes an interior gear driven mechanism to rotate the indicator needle on the face of the gauge in accordance with the correct depth. There are various types of depth gauges that utilize the Bourdon tube as the pressure sensing element.

1. *Open Bourdon Tube* — This type of Bourdon tube depth gauge allows the ambient sea water to enter the Bourdon tube, causing it to expand or contract in accordance with changes in depth. The diver's correct depth is then registered with the rotating needle on the face of the gauge.

With this type of gauge, it can often be difficult to insure that all the sea water or other foreign particles have been flushed from the interior of the tube after the dive. Only a very thorough rinsing, paying attention to the tiny openings in the Bourdon tube, will prevent this gauge from building up internal deposits that could cause inaccuracies.

OPEN BOURDON TUBE DEPTH GAUGE

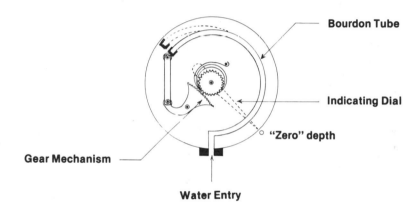

Bourdon Tube

Indicating Dial

"Zero" depth

Gear Mechanism

Water Entry

2. *Closed Bourdon Tube* — A closed Bourdon tube depth gauge uses a Bourdon tube that is filled with a fluid and sealed off at one end with a diaphragm. Ambient sea water acting on the diaphragm causes the Bourdon tube to register a change on the face of the gauge. This type of gauge is extremely simple to maintain, and a simple rinsing will suffice to keep it operating properly.

3. *Sealed Unit Bourdon Tube* — Another type of closed Bourdon tube depth gauge utilizes the Bourdon tube as a sealed unit, which is installed in its casing and then filled with a fluid. The case may have a diaphragm installed in it, or the case may be designed to provide its own medium for sensing a pressure change. The outside ambient water pressure transmits its pressure change to the fluid in the gauge, which causes the sealed Bourdon tube to expand or contract, according to the depth. These depth gauges are usually among the more expensive models, but they are also considered to be the most maintenance free and reliable.

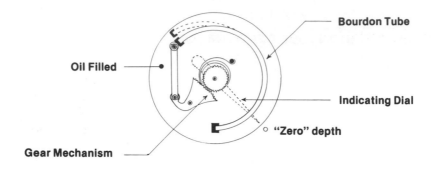

Piston Type Depth Gauges — The piston type depth gauge is similar to the capillary type. A straight tube in the housing is designed so that a small piston with an indicating mark on it may travel back and forth freely within the tube. When ambient water pressure enters the opening of the tube assembly, it acts upon the piston, causing it to move in the opposite direction. As the pressure increases, the water advances within the tube, and the indicating line on the piston registers the diver's depth. Piston type depth gauges must be rinsed very thoroughly after each dive to insure utmost accuracy. This gauge can be easily disassembled, the piston removed, and the interior can be flushed with fresh water.

SUBMERSIBLE PRESSURE GAUGES

Submersible pressure gauges are used to provide a constant reading of a diver's internal tank air pressure. Manufacturers regard submersible pressure gauges as *Factory Serviceable* instruments, and no repairs on the internal mechanisms of the gauges should be attempted by the sportdiver.

Whenever installing the regulator and gauge assembly, the submersible pressure gauge should be turned to face away from the diver. Then turn the air pressure on *slowly*, as damage could result if the air pressure is turned on too quickly. It could cause the glass or plastic lens to explode. After pressurizing the gauge, the gauge can be turned around to face the diver.

When contamination is suspected in a regulator, contamination may also be suspected in the pressure gauge. If salt water contamination is

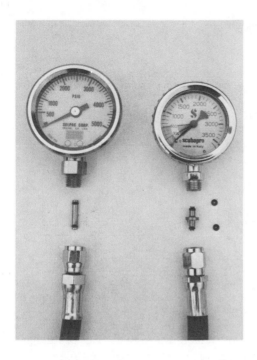

The restrictor orifice on the swivel assembly of the pressure gauge should be disassembled, cleaned and lubricated annually. The O-rings should also be replaced at this time.

suspected, it will be necessary to return the gauge to the manufacturer for repairs. Remove the gauge from the hose. Then rinse the high pressure hose and swivel assembly with distilled water, drying it thoroughly by using a clean, low pressure source of air.

Some submersible pressure gauges may also have internal lighting for use in situations of very restricted visibility or for night diving. The battery compartment on these gauges should be inspected periodically for any signs of corrosion.

When purchasing a submersible pressure gauge, the readings on the face of the gauge should be capable of indicating at least 5/3 of the working pressure of the scuba system with which it will be used. For example, for a 3,000 psi system, the gauge should be capable of reading pressures up to 5,000 psi. Even though lenses are removable on some types of gauges, it is recommended that they not be removed by the diver, due to the difficulty of getting the lens to seal properly when reassembled. Any time any work is done on a submersible pressure gauge, it must be disconnected from its air source.

Types of Gauges —

1. *Open Bourdon Tube* — This type of pressure gauge operates with a Bourdon tube as the pressure sensing mechanism. The air pressure from the tank enters the Bourdon tube, causing it to expand or contract as the

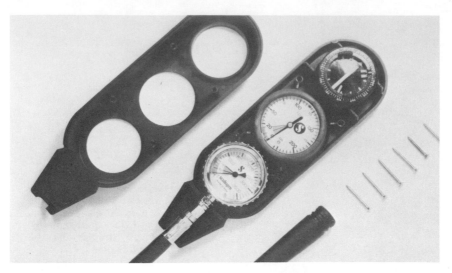

For added protection and greater convenience, most types of gauges can be installed in instrument consoles. Stainless steel screws should be used to facilitate in taking the console apart for periodic internal inspections.

pressure increases or decreases. This movement through a series of linkages causes the needle to register the tank pressure on the face of the gauge.

2. *Closed Bourdon Tube* — The air pressure from the tank completely surrounds the Bourdon tube assembly within the gauge. As the air pressure increases or decreases, the Bourdon tube will expand and contract, thus causing the needle to rotate. This type of gauge is generally depth compensated by the use of an oil filled boot which causes the Bourdon tube to also be affected by the increase or decrease in the surrounding water pressure as the diver's depth changes.

UNDERWATER COMPASSES

Routine maintenance for compasses should include a fresh water rinse, paying particular attention to the bezel ring. Always rotate the bezel ring while directing the flow of fresh water towards it. Some types of newer compasses can be completely disassembled, including the bezel ring, for a more complete rinsing.

Before using an underwater compass, always assure that the needle moves freely. Never leave a compass in direct sunlight, as the case can expand, causing the needle to come off of the compass. On compasses with a rotating bezel ring, sand can become lodged underneath them, causing them to freeze up, or to etch the lens on the compass face.

Installing Compasses — Whenever installing the compass on a compass board or within a console, assure that all attaching hardware is of non-ferrous metal, such as stainless steel or bronze. Steel can affect the accuracy

Automatic decompression meters should be stored and transported in special air-tight containers. This will give good protection from rough handling and from damage caused by altitude changes when traveling by air or in high altitude terrain.

of the compass. When installing compasses on consoles, assure that the other gauges do not impair their operation.

This can be done by testing the compass with the other gauges. Place the compass in an area with non-magnetic interference and let the needle stabilize itself. Then place the console with all of its hardware and other gauges installed in it next to the compass to observe the extent of magnetic interference, if any.

A sportdiver's compass work is normally used for general headings underwater. Since extreme accuracy is ordinarily not required, a little deviation of the needle may be acceptable. Don't store the compass around other compasses or next to anything which has a strong magnetic field, such as transformers.

AUTOMATIC DECOMPRESSION METERS

Automatic decompression meters are precision instruments, and should be treated accordingly. Rough handling, dropping, bumping, banging, and careless packing and storing can jar the mechanism and affect its accuracy. If a decompression meter is jarred or dropped, it should be tested again before the next dive. Automatic decompression meters should be routinely tested for accuracy *once every 6 months,* and preferably in a pressure chamber.

The meter should be rinsed with fresh water after every dive. Excessive exposure to sunlight or heat should be avoided. Assure that the meter is thoroughly dry before storing or sealing in a travel case. Heavy duty travel cases for decompression meters can be purchased from dive shops, or from the dealer. These are specially designed cases that protect the meter from rough handling and seal it in an air tight compartment to prevent damage caused by pressure changes, such as when traveling in mountainous areas or by plane. Exposure to high altitude will damage the meter.

Never attempt to disassemble or repair the decompression meter yourself. To rinse and flush sand and salt water from the interior of the case, the strap may be removed, if done so very carefully and gently.

Spearguns

Spearguns are designed to cater to a variety of spearfishing needs for the sportdiver, and are so differentiated in design and construction. From the simplest pole spear to the rugged big game gun, each diver chooses a speargun that will match the requirements of his particular type of underwater hunting. For added efficiency or versatility, many divers often acquire several different sizes of spearguns in order to be prepared for hunting in different types of underwater environments, or for different species of game.

There are over 100 different types of spearguns on the market today. However, most spearguns require the same basic type of care and maintenance, and also have similar design features. It is these basic features that will comprise the focal point of the following section, along with suggestions for do-it-yourself construction and repair projects, and recommendations for effective safety and maintenance habits.

SPEARSHAFTS

The most trouble-free spear shafts are those constructed of stainless steel, due to its corrosion resistant properties. Other types, which usually encompass the less expensive models, may be made of steel with a galvanized coating added for protection from corrosion. With the proper upkeep, steel shafts can last a long time. However, since the galvanization can mar or scratch and will eventually wear off after a period of prolonged use, spearguns with galvanized steel shafts require more maintenance and should be protected with a light coat of oil when not in use.

Shaft Size — The size of the spear shaft is one of the major distinguishing features among spearguns, since it is the size of the spear shaft that largely determines the size and strength of the fish that the speargun is capable of handling. Generally, the longer the spear shaft and the greater the diameter (within prescribed limits), the greater the range and impact of the speargun. The size and length of the rubber slings also plays a role in determining the force, range and impact of the gun.

Speargun shafts are currently available in three diameters — 1/4", 5/16" and 3/8". Smaller guns employ spear shafts of 1/4" diameter, since they can not produce enough thrust to propel larger shafts through the water. The smaller guns are the most inexpensive types, and are designed for close-range hunting of smaller game. The larger spearguns used by experienced spearfishermen utilize shafts of 5/16" and 3/8", since they are designed to deliver more speed and impact. These characteristics can change, however, when the speargun has been modified by changing the size or strength of the rubber slings.

Maintenance — When rinsing the spear shaft after a dive, inspect it carefully for any signs of wear or damage that it may have received while using it. The shaft should be free of any bends, nicks or galls, so that the slide will run the entire length of the shaft freely.

Inspect the threads for any defects. If the threads are damaged, they can be chased with the proper dye to clean them. If they are cracked or broken, the end of the spearshaft can be turned down on a lathe and rethreaded. Don't throw away a good spear shaft just because the threads are damaged.

Inspect the area around the sling notches for any bending or cracking. If the shaft breaks here, it can be welded together and ground smooth. Then, a new notch can be cut into the shaft using double hack saw blades in a hack saw frame. This new notch can be placed in the shaft slightly in front of or behind the spot where the original notch was located.

When storing the spearshaft, the spear tip should always be removed.

SPEARTIPS

There are several types of spear tips available for spearguns and pole spears, each one intended for a specialized function.

PITCH FORK SPEAR TIP

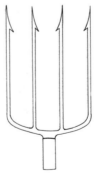

Pitch Fork Type — Used primarily on hand slings, or pole spears, this type is used for small game fish. The more barbs or points on the spear head, the more force will be required for penetration. This type dulls easily, and is designed to be used for game fish weighing up to five pounds.

PARALYZER SPEAR TIP

Paralyzer — (Hawaiian spear head) — The holding power of this type is a combination of penetration and spreading of the points which causes the tip to grip the fish. These tips should always be doubly sharpened so as to cause the points to penetrate to their maximum capacity. It is generally used for game fish weighing up to twelve pounds.

SINGLE BARB HEAD

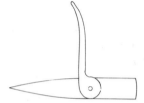

Single Barb Head — This type of spear tip incorporates a hinged barb which spreads after penetration. It is often difficult to remove from the fish. The best way to remove it without damaging it is to push it on through the fish, then unscrew the tip from the shaft and pull the shaft back through the fish. It is used on smaller spear guns or hand slings, and is recommended for fish weighing up to fifteen pounds.

DOUBLE BARB HEAD

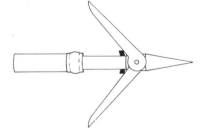

Double Barb Head — The double barb spear tip incorporates two hinged barbs which unfold in opposite directions after the fish has been speared, and thus aids in retaining the fish on the spear. These also have a retaining ring to aid in removal of the tip from the fish. By pushing the tip through the fish and sliding the ring over the barb, the shaft can be more easily removed from the fish.

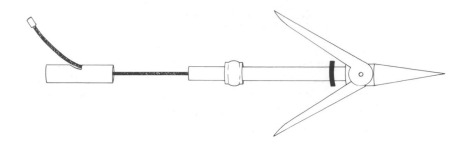

Detachable Spear Head — This type of spear tip utilizes a small piece of cable to connect the shaft and spear tip together once the spear tip has separated from the shaft. This makes it more difficult for the fish to pull the spear point out. If the small cable begins to fray, it can easily be replaced on most types of spear tips. Detachable spear heads are popularly used in guns with a shaft length of three feet or more.

General Maintenance — Regardless of the type of spear tip utilized for underwater hunting, it should always be kept as sharp as possible, and covered with a protector when not in use. A dull spear tip only wounds a fish and will not function in its intended capacity if not properly sharpened. Using a spear tip for prying or poking can not only dull the tip, but may also damage the spear shaft.

Always double check the tightness of the spear tip to the shaft. This can loosen easily, and come apart from the spear shaft, often unbeknownst to the diver. However, the tip should never be tightened while the shaft is mounted to the gun, as this can damage the trigger mechanism on the gun. The best way to tighten the spear tip is to hold the shaft in a soft jawed vice. This will not gall the shaft. Then carefully tighten the spear tip.

TRIGGER MECHANISMS AND HOUSING

Speargun trigger housings are made of either cast aluminum or plastic, while the inner safety and trigger mechanism themselves are made of stainless steel. The trigger and safety mechanisms should always operate freely and easily. If you notice any binding or hesitation of the mechanisms, rinse them thoroughly with a high pressure stream of warm water while activating the moving parts. If this does not alleviate the problem, then disassembly may be required.

No alterations should ever be made inside the trigger or safety mechanisms. Before loading a speargun, always insure that the safety mechanism works. To test the safety mechanism:

1. Install the shaft in the trigger mechanism. Do not attach slings.

2. Turn the safety to the on position.

3. Gently pull the trigger to see if the shaft releases, always keeping the speargun pointed away from yourself and other persons.

4. Now turn the safety to the off position, and again pull the trigger. The shaft should slide out.

Never use a speargun with a faulty trigger or safety mechanism.

RUBBER POWERED SPEARGUN

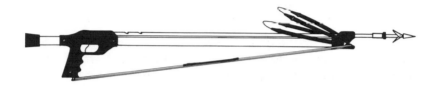

POLE SPEAR

LINES

The two most popularly used types of line for spearguns are nylon line and polypropylene line.

Polypropylene Line — is highly desirable due to its inherent strength and resistance to abrasion. It is resistant to rot and can be spliced without the aid of knots. It is also easy to untangle and does not kink.

Nylon Line — This type of line is also popular due to its strength and ability to stretch. It is highly resistant to rot, and stands up well under rugged use. Its stretchability also endows it with good shock absorbing qualities.

Stainless Steel — Stainless steel cable is often used in conjunction with nylon or polypropylene line. It is used on large guns as leaders, in order to prevent the fish from breaking the line near the spear shaft. Short pieces should be used as the cable tends to kink and also frays easily, making it somewhat difficult to work with underwater.

Shock Absorbers — Shock absorbers in the form of a small piece of rubber tubing are installed on the line in most professional quality guns to provide a shock absorbing effect when spearing. This prevents the spear point from being pulled out easily once the fish has run the entire length of the line. These should be inspected frequently for signs of rot and deterioration around the retaining rings.

To Install a Line and Shock Absorber — Select the proper type of line to be used. The length of the line will be determined by the size of the speargun. Roughly, the line should be about 4½ times the distance from the muzzle to the line release mechanism.

1. Attach the line to the spear shaft slide, using a bowline knot. Extend the line backwards toward the line release mechanism, and wrap it back and forth between the line release mechanism and the tip of the muzzle a total of four times.

BOWLINE KNOT

2. On the fourth wrap, as you are bringing the line forward from the line release mechanism to the muzzle of the gun, stop at a point on the line approximately 2/3 of the total distance away from the muzzle. Tie a regular granny knot in the line at this point in order to begin installing the shock absorber.

GRANNY KNOT

3. To install the shock absorber, select a piece of rubber tubing the desired length. This will depend upon the size of the speargun, but it is usually about six to eight inches in length. Take the free end of the nylon line not attached to the spear shaft slide, and slide the rubber tubing up the line until it reaches the point at which you have tied the granny knot.

4. Slide the tubing just slightly over the knot, and secure it in place behind the knot by using a retaining ring or a heavy duty Dacron or nylon thread or fishing line. (Have somebody else stretch the rubber while you hold the line. Then take ten or fifteen good wraps with the fishing line or thread over the rubber tubing just back of the original granny knot, and tie it off with a good square knot while the tubing is still outstretched.)

SQUARE KNOT

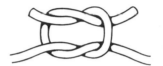

5. Tie another granny knot in the nylon or polypropylene line about six to eight inches forward of the free end of the rubber tubing. Then stretch the rubber tubing up to this knot. (*Hint:* Take hold of the free end of the tubing with one hand. With the other hand, hold the tubing where it has been secured to the line and stretch the tubing. This will advance the second knot to the free end of the rubber tubing.)

6. Extend the free end of the tubing slightly over the second granny knot, and secure it in the same manner as the first knot, with a retaining ring, or with Dacron thread or fishing line just behind the knot. Both knots will now be inside the rubber tubing, and when the tubing is relaxed, a length of line twice the length of the tubing will be wrapped inside. This will serve as a shock absorber.

7. After installing the shock absorber, extend the entire line forward to the muzzle. While keeping the line snug, but not stretching the shock absorber excessively, tie the line through the hole or ring provided on the muzzle and secure it with a strong bowline knot. Cut off any excess line.

SPEAR SLINGS

For maximum longevity and continued accuracy of a speargun, always use the size and strength of rubber slings recommended by the manufacturer. Overloading a speargun with more slings than the gun is designed to handle can lead to inaccuracies and can produce increased wear on the trigger mechanism. Trigger mechanisms may eventually wear down over a period of time, but increasing the strength of the slings on a gun will accelerate this process.

Using too many slings on a speargun can result in one of three possible malfunctions, which can create potentially dangerous situations for the diver or those around him:

1. The trigger sear may develop a rounded or worn surface in a critical area, which will cause the speargun to fire prematurely just as the last sling is being loaded. If the safety is on while you are loading the gun, this won't happen; but instead, it will fire the moment the safety is turned off rather than when you pull the trigger. Either way, a very dangerous situation could result.

2. The trigger sear can also develop burred surfaces, which can cause the speargun not to fire at all, no matter how hard you pull the trigger. Often, the speargun may fire only under extreme pressure or exertion on the trigger.

3. Too many slings on a speargun can also affect the accuracy of the shaft trajectory. When the gun is overloaded, the back portion of the shaft will have a tendency to gain more speed than the tip, and the shaft will oscillate (or vibrate in back and forth motions) along the length of the gun when the gun is fired. This is more likely to happen in guns with long and thin shafts.

Construct your own sling — Although professional dive shops carry replacement slings for spearguns, it may at one time or another be necessary to make your own sling for special applications or for field repairs. In order to do this, you will need to obtain the following materials: surgical tubing, sharp scissors, pliers, a "wishbone" and two "wishbone" rings or heavy duty Dacron thread.

Lengths of surgical tubing, either black or amber colored, can be purchased through most dive shops. To determine the proper length of a sling, a good rule of thumb to use is that the sling, when relaxed and affixed to the gun, should be about 1/3 the length of the spear shaft. To select the proper diameter of a sling, choose that which is recommended by the manufacturer or use the following guidelines:

1. Tubing of 3/8" diameter or less is used on most pole spears, and also as shock absorbers and on line assemblies of spearguns.

2. Tubing of 7/16" to 1/2" diameter is used on most popular sizes of spearguns, usually those under four feet in length.

3. For larger spearguns, over four feet in length, tubing of 9/16" diameter and larger is used.

Procedures for constructing a sling — Select the proper size of surgical tubing, and cut a few inches longer than the desired length. Using a pair of scissors, trim both ends of the tubing to a diagonal slant, to facilitate in

TO CONSTRUCT A SPEAR SLING

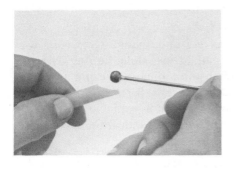

1. Trim the surgical tubing to a diagonal slant.

2. Install the wishbone and ring assembly onto the tubing.

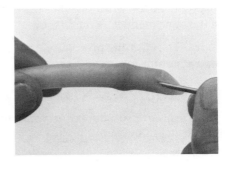

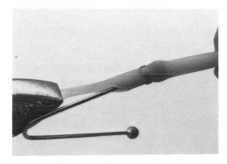

3. Secure the retaining rings over the wishbone and tubing.

4. Finish the sling by trimming the tubing straight across.

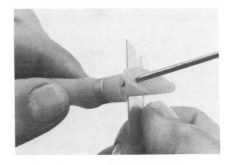

gripping the tubing and installing the wishbone ring.

1. Select the proper size wishbone and ring assembly. These are available at most professional dive shops.

2. Insert the ball on one end of the wishbone into one end of the tubing, pushing it down into the tubing about an inch.

3. Secure the tubing in a vise, or have a buddy hold it for you, at a point about two inches down from the ball. Now, slide the ring over the wishbone from the other end, and stretch the tubing out, using a pair of pliers. Slide the ring over the stretched tubing until it rests up against the ball inside the tubing. (*Hint:* If a retaining ring is not available, heavy duty Dacron thread or fishing line can be used to tie the surgical tubing in place just behind the ball on the wishbone.)

4. Place the second ring on the interior of the wishbone, and insert the other end of the wishbone into the other side of the surgical tubing. Secure in the same manner as the first one.

5. To finish the procedure, trim the ends of the surgical tubing straight across, cutting away the diagonal.

SPEARGUN MAINTENANCE

Clean-up procedures for your speargun assembly after diving should include the following:

1. Remove the spear shaft from the speargun. Remove the spear tip from the shaft.

2. Remove the rubber butt plug from the rear of the speargun assembly.

3. Rinse all parts thoroughly with fresh water, directing the flow of water into the trigger mechanisms. This should remove all traces of sand, salt or other particles from the interior of the gun.

4. Dry thoroughly. For storage, the slings may be given a light coat of silicone. Work it well into the rubber, then wipe off the excess. Surgical tubing should always be stored away from direct sunlight, and should be removed from the speargun when not in use. For maximum protection, they may be sealed in an airtight plastic bag.

5. The speargun itself, if galvanized steel, may be wiped with a light coat of oil (such as WD-40) to protect against corrosion. Never use heavy oil internally on the gun, as this may cause particles of sand or dirt to adhere to the interior, causing triggering malfunctions.

Note: For ease of cleaning and for protection from internal corrosion, two 3/8'' holes may be drilled into the bottom of the center tube approximately two inches from either end. This will facilitate the draining of sea water after the dive, while also providing access for a more thorough rinsing. In some spearguns, however, the center tube is sealed to provide buoyancy for the speargun. If you wish to retain this buoyancy, do not drill the holes.

ABOUT PNEUMATIC SPEARGUNS

Pneumatic spearguns are more sophisticated than rubber-powered spearguns, and the initial cost of purchasing one is somewhat higher. Pneumatic spearguns are powered by compressed air, that is pumped into the speargun and pressurized with a special, hand-operated pump. The expanding action of the compressed air acting on the piston powers the gun. Then, by reinserting the shaft and recompressing the piston inside the gun, the energy can be recovered and used over again. A pneumatic gun will usually need recharging about once a year, depending upon the frequency of use.

Maintenance — Routine maintenance for all pneumatic spearguns should include rinsing them after each dive. Abrasive materials and particles such as sand, should never be allowed to accumulate in the cylinder. In addition, they should be stored in a vertical position with the muzzle pointing down. This will help keep the piston seals oiled, so they won't dry out and become brittle.

All pneumatic spearguns contain a mixture of oil in with the compressed air to provide lubrication for the piston (which slides inside the cylinder) and for the trigger mechanism. The oil also helps reduce friction on the moving parts inside the gun, and helps insure the integrity of the O-ring seals which contain the compressed air. The oil should be changed at least once a year if the gun is frequently used, and once every other year for infrequent use. O-rings should also be inspected and changed, if necessary, when the oil is being changed.

Most manufacturers of pneumatic spearguns usually include detailed service instructions for the gun, as well as drawings and supply parts lists. These should be adhered to rigidly by the diver. Other manufacturers recommend that you send the speargun back to the factory at least every two years for cleaning, inspection and necessary maintenance operations. The speargun should be serviced in accordance with the manufacturer's recommendations.

SPEARGUN SAFETY

1. Insure that the trigger and safety mechanisms are functioning properly and as designed by the manufacturer.

2. Never shoot a speargun out of the water. This can damage the spear shaft and tip, and the shaft may ricochet dangerously in any direction.

3. Be aware of other divers while using a speargun underwater. Don't

fire it unless you are sure of your target.

4. Keep the speargun unloaded while not in use. Don't rely on the safety mechanism to keep the gun from firing. Trigger and safety mechanisms can wear out with prolonged use and handling over a period of years.

5. Always unload the speargun before entering a boat after diving, or before handing the speargun to someone else on the boat.

6. Do not overload the speargun with slings that are too short or too thick, or with excessive air pressure, in the case of pneumatic spearguns.

7. Do not load spearguns while beach diving until you are past the surf when entering the water. Always unload them prior to entering the surf line when exiting from the water. *Remember:* A speargun exerts a tremendous force and can be extremely dangerous when fired.

8. Always rinse your speargun thoroughly after a dive, and work the mechanisms to insure that they function properly.

9. Never load or shoot a speargun with a bent shaft. This can cause damage to the gun or to yourself or other persons.

Diving Knives

The numerous design features available in diving knives today allow divers to choose a knife that is tailored to suit their individual needs. There are all-purpose knives. There are knives designed for protection, for hunting and for cleaning game. And there are knives designed for cutting, scraping or sawing, as well as for poking, prying, pounding and hammering. Some models even sport built-in can openers, bottle openers and screwdrivers. For safety reasons alone, however, every diver should carry a knife underwater for such emergency situations as entanglements in kelp, netting, fishing line or any other constraints.

DESIGN FEATURES

With the wide variety of designs available, every diver should carefully assess his particular diving needs before purchasing a diving knife. By analyzing its intended use beforehand, the diving knife can be a personalized diving aid. If you're unsure of how you will be using your knife, then choose an all-purpose knife that you can carry along for safety reasons as well as miscellaneous uses that may arise.

Knife Tips — Diving knives run the gamut from dagger-like tips designed for piercing to broad, blunt tips designed for prying. A spearfisherman might choose a sharp tip for accurate piercing and for cleaning game, while a wreck diver might prefer a sturdy, blunt tip that could serve as a fulcrum for prying. A knife with a narrow blunt tip can also double as a screwdriver for minor equipment adjustments.

Knife Edges — The straight edge on a diving knife should always be kept sharply honed, since a sharp knife edge is safer than a dull one. A straight-edge knife is generally designed for all-purpose slicing or cutting, while serrated or saw-toothed edges aid in cutting or sawing through thicker materials or objects. Most diving knives incorporate a serrated edge along with a straight edge. Some knives are designed with a sharply notched groove cut into the blade for more efficient line cutting.

Knife Handles — Most dive knife handles are made of rubber or plastic in varying sizes and shapes. The dive knife handle should be easy to grip and provide a well-balanced feeling for the knife. Most handles contain a flat, broad stainless steel butt, that functions in a hammering capacity for underwater or topside use. If you will be wearing thick, neoprene gloves when using your knife underwater, take this into consideration and select a thicker or larger handle that is easier to grip with gloves.

Sheaths — Knife sheaths are a personal matter of preference. Most knives do come equipped with their own sheath to be strapped on to the diver's calf, thigh or arm. Some knives may fit into instrument consoles or special custom pockets in the diver's wetsuit or BC. Regardless of where the knife is located, it should be easily accessible, and preferably within easy reach of the diver's dominant hand. It should also provide a minimum amount of drag in the water and should not be placed where it may easily catch on passing kelp, coral or other possible entanglements.

DIVER'S KNIFE

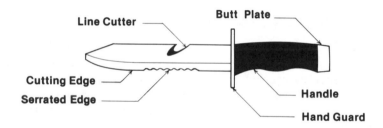

MAINTENANCE

As with other diving equipment, the dive knife should also be rinsed with fresh water after diving. Although most diving knives are made of corrosion-resistant stainless steel, some types of knives may still acquire a light coat of surface rust when stored. To minimize this, do not store the knives in a wet sheath. Make sure the sheath and knife are completely dry before placing the knife back inside its protective sheath. After washing and drying, a light coat of silicone spray or other rust preventative may be applied to the blade for storage.

Sharpening a Knife — Even though your dive knife may only be used for poking and prodding, it is still a valuable tool that may be required in order to cut through fishing line, netting or kelp. Because of its potential use in emergency situations, it should always be kept sharp and in good condition.

Sharpening a knife on a rough stone will usually suffice to keep a good edge on it. However, before sharpening, double check the manufacturer's recommendations. Some of the knives on the market are heavy plated chrome over a lesser grade of steel, and sharpening will destroy its rust barrier. It is not a good idea to maintain a razor sharp edge on an all-purpose knife, as you may accidentally cut yourself or your wetsuit while taking it in or out of its sheath or pocket. A grinding disc or wheel should never be used to sharpen a knife, as it could destroy the edge of the knife.

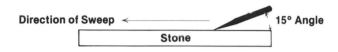

To Sharpen a Knife — Before sharpening, the knife should be rinsed with fresh water, and dried thoroughly with a clean cloth, paying particular attention to any grooves or crevices such as the line cutting notch and the serrated edges.

1. Coat the stone with a light coat of honing oil or machine oil. It is imperative that the stone be moistened first, and even saliva will do if some type of oil is not available.

2. Hold the knife edge so that its edge is at an approximate angle of 15° to the cutting surface of the stone.

3. Slide the knife across the stone in a sweeping motion from handle to tip, as if trying to slice off a piece of the stone. Turn the blade over and repeat this process on the other side of the blade, sweeping the knife across the stone in the opposite direction. Repeat while alternating sides, one stroke at a time, until the knife exhibits a good sharp edge.

4. To obtain a good sharp edge, it is important that you keep the knife blade on both sides at the same angle that you started with.

5. If the knife has nicks or an extremely dull edge, sharpen the blade on a rough stone first, and then finish up on a fine stone. To give an even finger sharp edge, use a sharpening steel to dress the edge after the knife has been stone sharpened.

About Fillet Knives — Fillet knives may be made of either stainless steel or carbon steel. To prevent rust, they should be oiled and installed into their dry sheath after thoroughly washing and wiping dry with a clean cloth. Fillet knives are brittle and break easily. The tip of a fillet knife should never be used for prying or poking. They are extremely sharp instruments and should be handled accordingly.

Weight Systems

Initially, nylon or rubber belts sporting lead weights of various sizes comprised just about the only choice divers had for weighting themselves properly. But today, the standard weight belt has given way to other types of weight systems, largely as a result of the introduction of the back flotation units for buoyancy control. Now divers have a choice of wearing their weights on their backs or around the middle, as a separate piece of gear or incorporated into the tank or backpack. Even the weights themselves are available in a vivid array of colors, shapes and sizes.

Divers usually weight themselves in accordance with their individual diving pursuits. The proper amount of weight should, ideally, counteract or inhibit any undesirable amount of flotation underwater, so the diver can accomplish his diving objectives with a minimum amount of exertion. Whatever type of weight set-up you choose, it should be routinely maintained so that the weights can be dropped freely and easily with one hand should the need arise in an emergency situation.

WEIGHT BELTS

Some type of waist belt with affixed weights is the traditional set-up for diving weights. The belt material may consist of nylon webbing in assorted colors, or of black rubber, or it may be a combination of nylon webbing with an expandable rubber insert. An alternative type of waist belt called the shot belt is comprised of vinyl rubber with several compartments filled with BB shot. The shot belt conforms to the shape of the diver for more comfort, and eliminates the bulk and awkwardness that solid weights may produce.

Trimming belts — Before trimming a belt, it is best to suit up with all of your equipment to determine how it will fit in relation to other gear that you will be wearing underwater. This will make it easier to determine the correct length to be trimmed. Then affix all of the weights, clips and other equipment that you may be mounting to your belt, making sure they are located in a comfortable position. Remember: anything that you might attach to your weight belt should be expendable, since you may have to drop your weight belt at a moment's notice. It is not a good idea to let expensive gauges or other vital equipment hang from your weight belt.

After determining the proper fit of the belt, leave about six to eight inches of excess belt at the point the belt leaves the buckle, in order to be able to adjust the belt easily with gloves on underwater. With expandable belts, make sure that the belt fits snugly without undue stretching of the rubber before positioning the buckle or trimming any excess.

To cut the nylon webbing, use a very sharp pair of scissors or a single edged razor blade. Cut the belt in a rounded edge. This will aid in positioning the belt in the buckle, since it is easier to thread a rounded edge than a square edge. Use a hot soldering iron or a match flame to melt the end of the nylon webbing, thus fusing the nylon fiber together to prevent fraying and unraveling. Be careful to avoid contact with the hot, melted nylon.

Buckles — There are generally two types of weight belt buckles: the standard quick release buckle, such as the type found on tank waist strap buckles, and a wire frame quick release buckle. The wire frame quick release buckle functions most efficiently on expandable belts that contract underwater as the wetsuit compresses, since the buckle cannot be used to take up the slack. Some manufacturers have put a large notch in the metal release mechanism of the standard buckles to aid the diver in distinguishing between his tank buckle and his weight belt buckle.

Even though buckles are made of stainless steel, they are not as indestructible as most divers believe. A safe weight belt should always have a quick release mechanism that will operate easily to drop the weights should the need arise. Dropping weight belts carelessly on boat decks or laying tanks on top of them can cause the buckles to become distorted. Usually, they can be straightened out again with pliers, but if badly bent they may have to be replaced before the next dive.

Always inspect the hinges and attached points on the buckles for any signs of wear or distortion before the dive. Sometimes the ears or flanges may become distorted and the hasp will fall out. Simply bending the ear back down over the hinge pin will prevent this. On buckles with hinge pins, inspect the clips which keep the pin in place for security. It is always a good idea to carry an extra buckle with you on dive trips of any extended duration, for either your weight belt or your tank waist band.

PROPER THREADING OF QUICK RELEASE BUCKLE ASSEMBLY

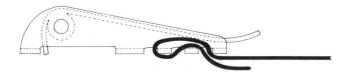

Weights — Various shapes and sizes of lead weights, ranging from one-pound bullet-shaped weights to ten-pound contoured hip weights, are used by divers. The choice is a matter of individual preference. Some divers prefer to use a pair of ten-pound contoured hip weights, while others find it easier to handle four or five smaller weights. Still others prefer the comfort of the shot belt, with its conforming fit and lack of protruding weights. In addition to the difference in shape and size, there are also vinyl-coated weights, which not only add extra color for photography and personal identification but also minimize damage to surrounding surfaces such as boat decks, swimming pools and other diving equipment.

Once the proper amount of weight has been determined, the weights should be affixed securely in place to prevent sliding while underwater or while removing the belt. Many a diver has handed his weight belt up to a buddy on the dive boat only to see all of the weights come slipping past him into the water simply because he used the wrong end for handling and forgot to secure the weights to the belt. However, the more permanent the weights are attached to the belt, the harder it will be to make future adjustments, such as for wearing different wetsuits. Traveling divers usually prefer to use various weights of smaller sizes that are easy to adjust, so they can compensate quickly for wearing different wetsuits to dive in cooler or warmer waters.

Affixing Weights — There are various ways in which weights can be affixed securely to the weight belt:

1. Weight clips, sold through dive shops, are excellent to use for securing weights and are fairly easy to adjust when removing or adding weights. Clips should be placed on each side of the weights where slippage is undesirable. Regardless of the number of weights you use, it is always imperative that at least one clip be placed in front of the weight nearest to the excess end of the belt. This will prevent all of the weights from slipping off the belt.

2. An alternate method of securing weights is to put a half twist in the belt as it is threaded through the weight. This will only work with block weights that are slotted. This will prevent slippage as well as making it easy to change weights at a later date.

3. If the weights are to be positioned permanently and you don't anticipate any changes in your diving habits, then the weights may be secured by drilling a 1/8'' hole in the lead weight approximately 1/2'' deep. Then a sheet metal screw and washer (#8 sheet metal brass or stainless steel screw) may be screwed through the webbing and into the weight. This is a very secure way to affix your weights to the belt, but keep in mind that it will be difficult to adjust the weights to compensate for different situations.

WEIGHTS FOR BACK MOUNTED BC'S

Block weights, disc weights or ball shot and marbles are used in several types of weight systems that are carried on the diver's tank backpack or on the sides of the tank itself. The At Pak system and other similar type systems incorporate the weights in the tank backpack. The weights can be released by pulling a pin on the bottom of the tank pack. Even though marbles are used with the ball shot to prevent the shot from congealing together from corrosion, the weight compartment should always be rinsed thoroughly after every dive to prevent salt build up.

Some divers carry their weights on their tank, rather than around their waist. This has the advantage of eliminating two sets of straps in front and also moves the weights higher up on the body. Special units attached to the outside of the tank are filled with disc weights or block weights, and can usually be adjusted to ride either high or low on the tank for individual preferences for center of gravity. These weights are also released by pulling a ring or pin on the unit which opens the compartment and allows the weights to slip out. The weights and the interior of the units should also be rinsed thoroughly after diving to prevent salt build up.

MAINTENANCE

Weight systems are rugged pieces of equipment, and require little maintenance other than a fresh water rinse to eliminate salt build up. With weight belts, careful attention to the operating condition of the buckles is important. They should be quick release type buckles that operate freely and easily with one hand.

A buckle that falls apart underwater or opens by itself can create a dangerous situation. With back mounted weights, it is important that the weights in the sealed compartments are always rinsed thoroughly to prevent corrosion from salt build up. The pins should be pulled in order to rinse the weights and compartment after the dive to make sure they are operating as designed.

Underwater Dive Lights

The underwater dive light is one of the most versatile pieces of equipment that a diver can own. It is, of course, an absolute must for night diving, cave diving, and some types of underwater hunting and wreck diving. However, more and more divers are realizing the advantages of using lights during the daytime for sightseeing purposes, in order to light up the dark recesses of caves and crevices, or to simply "recapture" those colors that have disappeared due to the filtering effects of depth. For poor visibility and murky water conditions, a dive light aids in navigation as well as sightseeing. And dive lights are increasingly being used as aids in underwater photography to zero in on the subject for better focusing and lighting techniques.

Aside from underwater utilization, the dive light also functions as a reliable outdoor light for camping and boating, or for use in a car or recreational vehicle. It is durable, rugged and waterproof, and when properly maintained can be valuable in any number of emergency situations. To derive the maximum degree of dependability from your dive light, assure that it is always in good working order, ready to serve you in any situation.

TYPES OF UNDERWATER DIVE LIGHTS

There are a wide variety of lights available for the diver to consider. Some are brighter than others, some last longer than others and some cost more than others. Every diver should choose a light that will suit his particular diving needs, taking into consideration such factors as cost, what the light will be used for, how long the batteries or charge will last, how bright the light output is, and whether it can be easily serviced if something goes wrong. Underwater dive lights fall into two categories, according to the power supply from which they operate — those that use disposable batteries and those that use rechargeable batteries.

Disposable Batteries — Underwater dive lights that use disposable batteries are generally the least expensive to purchase initially, although the cost of replacing batteries over a long period of time should also be taken into consideration as part of the total cost. Three basic types of disposable batteries are used in underwater dive lights: the standard carbon-zinc batteries, heavy-duty carbon-zinc batteries, and alkaline batteries. Standard carbon-zinc batteries are the cheapest to use, but are considered poor performers when compared with the other types. Heavy-duty carbon-zinc batteries can outperform the standard carbon-zincs, but the best performers in terms of light output and service are the alkaline batteries, which also happen to be the most expensive ones.

When using alkaline batteries, however, be aware that not all lamps in underwater lights can accommodate the extra strength of alkaline batteries. Alkaline batteries produce a spike voltage, or an extremely rapid initial surge of power once the light is switched on. This power surge can burn out a bulb that is not designed for it. To compensate for this, some manufacturers recommend that you use one or two partially used standard carbon-zinc batteries along with the other alkalines in the battery pack. This will effectively dampen the initial surge voltage, thus enhancing the life of the bulb.

Rechargeable Batteries — Underwater dive lights that use rechargeable batteries include the most expensive models on the market. Divers who use an underwater light very frequently generally choose the rechargeable type, in order to save the long term expense of replacing batteries. However, the light duration as well as the charging time for rechargeable batteries should also be taken into consideration with your diving plans. Some rechargeable batteries can take up to 20 hours for a full recharge, and when coupled with a short light duration can severely limit the immediate repetitive use of your light. Currently, the majority of rechargeables last from between one to two hours of continuous use, which is more sufficient for a single dive but may limit repetitive dives.

Divers who travel frequently will also have to take into consideration the availability of electrical power for recharging purposes. Remote areas often preclude the use of rechargeable lights, unless you bring a supply of fully charged battery packs with you. Another option for dive trips to remote areas with a small boat, car or recreational vehicle is to use a charging unit that can be powered by 12 volts, D.C. and is designed to plug into an ordinary cigarette lighter socket. For travel abroad, a 240 volt, A.C. charger will usually be required, or you can purchase a converter for your regulator 110 volt, A.C. charger.

Conversions — Several major manufacturers offer a variety of "modular" lights, for those divers who may want to start out with disposable batteries and move up to a more powerful light later on. The modular feature allows for the use of less expensive disposable batteries that can be substituted with a more powerful rechargeable battery pack in the same housing whenever desired. To accomplish this conversion, however, in many cases the bulb should also be changed, since moving to a higher voltage may drastically reduce the life of the bulb.

An alternate option to consider if you own a light with disposable batteries and would prefer to have a rechargeable light is to carry out the conversion on the existing light yourself. This will save you the expense of purchasing a new rechargeable light. General Electric presently markets a rechargeable battery system called Perma-Cell (available at most department stores), which will allow you to convert your dive light from disposable to rechargeable batteries. Perma-Cell battery packs can be used in most lights having the same size disposable battery, as long as the bulb allows for the conversion. While a Perma-Cell unit may be an improvement over disposable batteries, particularly money-wise, they generally do not measure up to the capacity and performance of a similar type battery pack provided by dive light manufacturers.

PREVENTATIVE MAINTENANCE

Routine maintenance on any type of underwater light should include careful handling and a fresh water rinse and thorough drying after the dive. In addition, the following maintenance procedures can also help enhance the life and performance of your underwater dive light.

Batteries — Always check out the light before the dive. If the color of the light exhibits a yellow-orange shade, this is a sign that batteries should be replaced or recharged. After installing new batteries, test the light to assure that all of the batteries are functioning properly and that you have installed them correctly. Shake the batteries to make sure the light is not going to flicker before you seal the housing. In a light that uses multiple dry cells, it is a good idea to wrap the battery pack with tape or install rubber bands around the pack to insure that the batteries maintain good connection during use.

Disposable Batteries — Remove disposable batteries from the dive light prior to storage for any length of time, as they may begin corroding and cause damage to the interior of the light. Corroding batteries can also cause the internal pressure of the housing to build up excessively, causing the O-ring seal to squeeze outward or become distorted. This could lead to flooding on the next dive. It is best to take the batteries out of the light, leaving the lens loose and relaxed when not in use. Batteries are extremely susceptible to heat damage, and should always be stored away from direct sunlight or other hot areas.

Rechargeable Batteries — Do not store rechargeable batteries in a discharged state, and once stored, they should not be allowed to become deeply discharged through lack of use. Always follow the manufacturer's recommendations for recharging your light prior to storage. Most manufacturers will recommend recharging the battery after using it, and then further recharging the battery at periodic intervals when not in use. Handle rechargeable batteries cautiously. They are capable of producing high electrical current that could cause serious bodily injury. Do not touch the uninsulated battery leads with any part of your bare skin, and be careful if using any metal objects around the battery.

BULBS

The bulb in an underwater dive light is the most delicate component of the light assembly. The tiny filament inside the bulb is extremely fragile, and can be easily damaged by rough handling, such as dropping it or allowing it to bang against hard surfaces. A dive light should *never* be used as a hammer for pounding or prying. To protect the bulb and the light, wrap it in some type of protective material (clothing, towels, or a wetsuit) while transporting it to the dive site. (*Hint:* Obtain some scraps of neoprene and wetsuit cement from your dive shop to construct your own dive light protective case. This will not only protect the interior components of the light, but will also protect the lens from nicks and scratches.)

To Install Bulbs — To install most conventional bulbs in dive lights, hold the bulb by its base and clean the glass thoroughly with tissue. This should remove all fingerprints and dirt that could produce a hot spot in the bulb, causing it to fail on a future dive. While installing, use a piece of tissue to hold the bulb. Don't overtighten or twist the bulb excessively. Always avoid handling bulbs with your bare fingers.

If the interior compartment of your dive light so allows, extra bulbs can often be stored within the dive light. They should be wrapped in tissue paper and taped securely to prevent any damage. This will insure having an extra bulb available when one burns out.

Replacing Bulbs — Over a period of extended use, the glass of a conventional bulb will develop a black coating on the inside surface, due to the gradual vaporization of the bulb filaments. As this coating slowly builds up, the light output will steadily diminish. When this happens, it is time to replace the bulb. Halogen bulbs are less susceptible to such deposits, since the halogen gas inside acts as a retarding agent.

REFLECTORS

The surface of a reflector will tarnish very easily. Reflectors should not be cleaned or touched with bare fingers on either side of the reflective surface, since normal body acids or sweat will etch the surface. Whenever the reflector is removed from the light, it should be placed face down so dust and foreign matter can not collect on the interior reflective surface. When storing the light with the reflector inside the light, always set the light so the reflector is facing upward. This will prevent any chemical "sweating" or moisture inside the light from accumulating on the reflector.

Do not try wiping dust and foreign matter away from the reflective surface, as this will scratch the surface and can cause loss of brightness in the

Batteries in dive lights can be wrapped with tape or secured with rubber bands to insure a good connection. A spare bulb wrapped in tissue paper can also be stored in an empty space in the battery compartment, such as in the hollow opening that runs through the center of some battery casings.

light output. The surface can be cleaned by blowing any dust off with a stream of low pressure air, such as that used to clean photographic film. A delicate, photographic lens cleaning brush may also be used lightly.

SWITCHES

When preparing for a dive, it is a good idea to tape the switch to the off position. This small precaution will prevent it from being accidentally knocked or jarred to the on position, thus using up the batteries before the dive. Some dive lights already incorporate some type of locking device for the switch.

After diving, rinse the light thoroughly in fresh water, directing a low pressure stream of water in the switch assembly. This will clean out any foreign matter, grit or sand that may have accumulated under the switch. Operate the switch while rinsing. Switches that protrude through the housings should have the O-ring seals lubricated periodically, depending upon the frequency of use.

HOUSINGS

Plastic housings should be rinsed with fresh water after diving. Aluminum housings should be soaked in fresh warm water, then dried thoroughly and wiped with a thin film of light oil to prevent corrosion from "lifting" off the protective coating. If any chipping or cracking of the paint is noticed around the O-ring seat, the light should not be used until all of the paint is removed from the seat. This will insure a watertight seal. A good epoxy or enamel paint stripper will usually remove the paint. *(Hint:* Tape all areas not to be stripped with aluminum tape, and then strip affected area with a small aluminum brush. Be cautious with the stripper. Wear gloves and avoid splashing around the face and eyes.)

Whenever opening the housing of an underwater light, be careful not to allow any drops of sea water to enter the interior. Inspect all of the O-rings or sealing surfaces for signs of deterioration or dirt particles, and replace them whenever necessary. Before closing the housing back up, check to see that no wires are protruding, and that all components are installed properly. The O-rings should be cleaned and lightly lubricated with silicone before closing the housing. If the housing is difficult to close, check to make sure that you have not pinched the O-ring.

CORROSION

There are two types of corrosion that may occur in the interior of your underwater light:

1. Acid Corrosion — This can be caused by the acid which is produced as a result of chemical reactions within the batteries. This can happen whenever batteries are leaking inside the light.

2. Salt Water — Corrosion can also form as a result of salt water contamination in the interior, such as when changing batteries and allowing salt water drops to enter the interior.

Treatment of Corrosion — Both types of corrosion may be treated by using the following procedure:

1. Use fine sandpaper or a small wire brush to clean the affected area. Then neutralize the area with a paste made of baking soda and water.

2. Apply the baking soda/water paste to the affected area, and let it sit for about ten minutes. Then wipe off the paste and rinse thoroughly with fresh water.

3. Dry thoroughly. This will work on electrical contacts as well as housings.

FLOODED LIGHTS

Fast action is the greatest help in saving a flooded dive light. Turn off the light immediately and return to the surface. Get back to the boat or to a dry area to examine the light.

1. Drain out all of the sea water from the interior. Rinse the interior, including the bulb and batteries, with fresh water.

2. Follow the fresh water rinse with a final rinse in a solution of water and isopropyl alcohol, to aid in evaporating the moisture for a final drying. Drain thoroughly from the light all traces of water.

3. Using a mild heat or blowing source, such as a hair dryer or a scuba tank, dry the light as quickly as possible. With dry hands, reassemble the light, and try to determine the source of the flooding. Are there any distorted O-rings or deteriorated seals or cracks in the housing? Replace all worn or damaged items.

4. After all components in the light are dry, and the light is properly reassembled, turn the light on to test it. If it does not function, replace or recharge the batteries and try again. If malfunctions persist, return it to the manufacturer, with a note explaining the nature of the damage.

Underwater Photography Equipment

The popularity of underwater photography has experienced a tremendous boom in the last decade. Whether you take pictures once a year with a housed instamatic, or whether your main diving pursuit is photography, the first piece of camera gear you purchase is usually only the beginning of a considerable investment in time and money. Because underwater photography equipment is both fragile and expensive, the basics of proper care and maintenance are equally as important as a working knowledge of the equipment itself.

Most flooded cameras and other malfunctions can be traced to careless handling and sloppy maintenance, rather than to manufacturing defects. Always test new equipment before the dive to become thoroughly familiar with all controls and mechanisms. Check out housings, cameras or strobes in a swimming pool, taking the opportunity to shoot several rolls of test film to establish reliable distance settings and guide numbers. If internal malfunctions are suspected, have the equipment checked out by a qualified camera repairman who has the tools and skills required to disassemble the delicate inner mechanisms of your camera or strobe.

BEFORE THE DIVE

Develop a mental checklist or "inspection" of your entire photographic system before you enter the water. This is one of the most important habits you can develop to insure trouble-free photography underwater.

1. *Check* all camera settings before closing the housings. Is the camera loaded with film? Has the proper shutter speed or ASA number been set?

2. *Inspect* all submersible equipment for proper sealing of O-rings, to insure that nothing is obstructing the seals. When closing a housing with latches, close opposite latches simultaneously to insure even sealing.

3. *Test* your light source. Shoot the first couple of frames to make sure that the strobe or flash discharges correctly.

4. *Don't* rush. Never let a buddy or dive master rush you into the water before you are certain that your camera system has been carefully checked over.

5. *Check* your buddy out concerning the proper way to handle the equipment if he will be handing it down to you from the stern of a boat. When easing equipment into the water with a lanyard, make sure knots are doubly secure.

6. *Handle* camera equipment carefully. Although many advances have been made in the materials used in underwater equipment, they are still not completely "diver-proof." Don't let equipment slide around on the decks of boats, and don't use it to fend off rocks and coral heads.

7. *Once* underwater, look into the viewfinder, lens port, or strobe dome for early signs of leakage. If any water is detected in the housing, surface immediately, holding the most critical part of the equipment towards the surface to enable water to collect below it.

AFTER THE DIVE

Whether you use a popular 35mm camera in an underwater housing or a self-contained Nikonos underwater camera, clean up procedures after the dive should include:

1. Rinse the entire camera system thoroughly in fresh water at the earliest available opportunity after the dive. If camera equipment has been allowed to dry without proper washing, it should be *soaked* for 15 to 20 minutes in a tub of luke warm water as soon as possible. This will cause the salt crystals from even the smallest crevices to dissolve back into solution.

2. While rinsing, be careful not to force a high pressure stream of water on any of the O-ring seals, as this could cause leakage to the interior.

3. After rinsing, pat dry with an absorbant cloth until all water beads are absorbed. Remove connectors for light sources after the camera is dry. Do not leave connectors in the camera for extended periods of time, as they could become corroded, causing damage to the sync port threads.

4. Use dry surroundings for unloading or loading film. When reloading between dives, unseal the camera or housing very carefully, keeping in mind that residual water drops collected around the O-rings could enter the camera body interior.

5. After the equipment has been rinsed and completely dried, remove, clean and inspect the main camera or housing O-ring seals. Check for any signs of nicks, cracks or other defects, and replace if necessary.

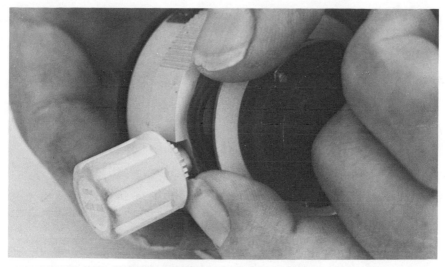

The best method of removing large O-rings from the groove is by applying pressure with the fingers while sliding the O-ring forward. Then insert a pencil or ball point pen under the O-ring and gently lift it from its groove. Never use sharp instruments to pry O-rings loose from their grooves.

O-RING MAINTENANCE

Removal — The best way to remove a large O-ring from its groove is to press against the edges of the O-ring seal very tightly with two fingers while simultaneously sliding the O-ring in the groove towards a convergent point. This will cause a loop to form as the rubber stretches, and a pencil or ball point pen can be inserted to keep the rubber from returning to the groove.

For smaller O-rings, try inserting a toothpick or any other similiar small instrument with dull or rounded edges. Do not try to lift or force the O-ring from its groove with sharp or pointed instruments, as it may damage the O-ring or scratch the sealing surface behind it.

Cleaning — O-rings may be cleaned with a soft, dry lint-free cloth by pulling the O-ring through the cloth gently until all dirt and grease have been removed. After cleaning, inspect the O-ring for signs of cracks or brittleness.

Clean O-ring grooves with a toothbrush and cotton swab to remove any dirt particles or excess grease. Take care to remove any remaining lint particles that the cotton swab may have left in the groove. To lubricate the O-ring, apply a small amount of silicone grease on a fingertip. Then pull the O-ring through your fingertips until a very light coat of grease has been evenly distributed on the O-ring surface.

Installing — When installing O-rings, take care not to get any grease on any of the lenses or lens ports, as it is very difficult to remove. Always select the proper size O-ring for the proper corresponding groove. Small O-rings should never be stretched to fit a larger groove, as they are not designed to function effectively when stretched beyond their normal size.

Keep extra O-rings in your spare parts kits in order to replace them when needed. When in doubt about the condition of an O-ring, replace it. O-rings are far less expensive than having to pay for repairs to your camera should faulty O-rings cause leakage.

FOR NIKONOS USERS

The Nikonos amphibious camera is currently the most popular self-contained submarine camera of a 35mm format on the market. It has a wide variety of lenses and accessories available for it and is extremely popular with underwater photographers. In addition to following routine rinsing procedures after the dive, Nikonos maintenance should also include special attention to other unique features of the camera.

O-rings — O-rings around the main camera body and lens should be given a good cleaning after each dive. Unseal the lens very carefully to prevent residual water drops from entering the interior. Periodically check the rewind lever O-ring. If the lever feels stiff and difficult to wind, lubricate the O-ring by applying a small amount of grease on the lever shaft and moving it up and down in its slot.

Sync Port — If you use a strobe or flash unit with your Nikonos, develop the habit of rinsing the camera and strobe unit as a whole before disconnecting them. This way you won't risk forgetting to replace the sync port plug in the camera body when rinsing it.

Inspect the strobe contacts in the sync port of the camera body for any signs of corrosion. If corrosion begins to accumulate, scrub the contacts with a light abrasive material. (The eraser tip of a typewriter pencil-type eraser works well. Fine sandpaper wrapped around a pencil tip can also be used, but use it cautiously, as it is more abrasive than an eraser). Clean the sync port with a soft brush to remove any particles left from cleaning away the corrosion.

If the threads have been stripped in the sync port, you need not replace the entire outer camera body. A threaded insert can be installed in a bored out sync port that will function just as well as the original.

Lens Care — Keep the front port of the Nikonos lenses free of spots by washing with fresh water. Dry the surface with a soft, lint-free cloth. To remove fingerprints from the lens use a good lens cleaner solution applied with a commercial lens cleaning tissue. Apply the lens cleaner with the tissue. Never pour it directly onto the lens, as the solution can seep down around the sides of the lens surface.

Since fingerprints contain body acids that may permanently etch glass, always remove fingerprint smudges immediately. If they are difficult to remove with lens tissue, try using a cotton swab lightly dampened with alcohol or lens cleaning solution. Use an easy, circular motion over the lens, but do not rub too vigorously.

Storage — When not in use, the Nikonos camera should be stored with the lens removed, and the outer and inner camera body separated. This will remove pressure from the O-rings, allowing them to last longer and seal effectively when reassembled. Leave the shutter uncocked. This will give the shutter springs both longer life and prolonged accuracy.

When storing a Nikonos for a prolonged period of time, use a soft cloth to apply a light coat of WD-40 to the camera body. Place the camera body in a closed container or plastic bag. A small packet of silica gel may be placed inside the body to insure dryness. Don't leave film in the camera for extended periods of time.

UNDERWATER HOUSINGS

If you own a popular camera or strobe, the chances are very good that there is either a housing available for it on the market, or one in the planning stages on a manufacturer's drawing board. Underwater housings can be constructed of virtually any material that satisfies certain watertight requirements under pressure. However, the two most popular types of material used in the commercial production of housings are durable varieties of plastic and metal.

WIRE BULKHEAD FITTING FOR HOUSING

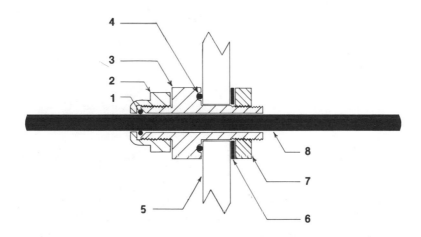

1. O-ring 2. Packing Nut 3. Bulkhead Fitting 4. O-ring 5. Housing 6. Washer 7. Nut 8. Wire.

Metal Housings — After drying with an absorbent cloth, metal housings may be wiped down with a light coat of oil (WD-40), taking care to apply it with a non-abrasive cloth. Never spray a lubricant on the housing, as you may risk spraying it on the lens port, where it is difficult to remove.

Metal housings require special attention to cleaning around the control seals and latch assemblies, due to the possibility of electrolysis. (Electrolysis is a corrosion process caused by the reaction of salt water with dissimilar metals, such as steel latches on an aluminum housing.) Pay particular attention to the tiny set screws which hold the housing knobs and triggers secure to their control shafts. Lubricate with a light coat of oil after drying.

Plastic Housings — Use plexiglass cleaner or polish, or a mixture of mild soap and water to clean smudges and spots from the housing. Be sure and rinse away any excess soap. Never use oil, solvents, or household window cleaners on plastic housings.

Check control knobs for stiffness. It is normal for these controls to stiffen up at depths, so test for stiffness when you have the housing out of the water. If the controls seem difficult to operate, it is time to lubricate them.

TYPICAL HOUSING CONTROL ASSEMBLY

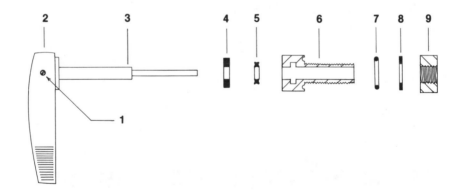

1. Set Screw 2. Knob 3. Control Rod 4. Washer 5. Seal 6. Bulkhead Fitting
7. O-ring 8. Washer 9. Nut

Lubricating Control Shaft Seals — An easy way to lubricate the control shaft seals on housings is to first extend the control shaft all the way out of the housing. Then, cover the extended part of the control shaft with a light coat of silicone grease. Slide the control shaft back into the housing. This will leave a sufficient amount of grease on the O-ring. Wipe away any excess grease.

Do not use this shortcut as a substitute for periodically removing and cleaning or replacing the control seals when necessary. Always inspect the controls for any signs of corrosion that may need to be removed.

Cleaning Control Seals — Depending upon the frequency with which you subject your housing to salt water, you should periodically remove and clean (or replace) the seals around the control assemblies. Never attempt to remove and clean a seal unless you have a replacement for it.

1. Remove the knob or control from the control shaft. Inspect the end of the shaft for any nicks or burrs that could cut the seal on the way out. (Lightly file or sand down if you find any rough edges.)

2. With a small, dull instrument remove the seal from its groove. Clean the seal and inspect for any damage. Lubricate the O-ring with silicone grease and fit it into the control shaft hole, pushing it gently down into the control sleeve until it slips into the seal groove. (This may require several tries.)

3. Lubricate the shaft with silicone grease and reinstall. Reinstall the control levers or knobs. Give the housing a pressure check with no equipment in it before using.

Cracks, Nicks and Scratches — If you discover a crack in your underwater housing, return it immediately to the manufacturer for replacement or repair. Never dive with even the smallest crack in your underwater housing.

Deep scratches and nicks may cause what is known as a stress riser (a starting place for a crack to begin as the housing contracts and expands under pressures caused by depth). If the watertight integrity of the housing is under question, the best course of action is to return it to the manufacturer for further action.

With time and frequent use, you will most likely accumulate a few small scratches on the external surface of the lens port. These are generally tolerable if they are small, since they tend to fill with water and will produce no serious distortion or blemishes on the final photograph.

Heavy scratches may be polished out, using one of the plexiglass scratch removal kits designed for use on aircraft windshields. Small scratches or even coarse polish marks on the inside of the lens port will definitely show up on the photograph and should be polished out. If the scratches prove stubborn, the lens must be replaced.

LIGHT SOURCE CONNECTORS

When cleaning a camera housing, always inspect for signs of corrosion around the light source connector units. If corrosion is detected, take immediate steps to remove it.

EO (Electro-Oceanic) CONNECTOR

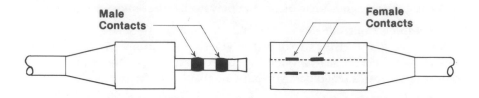

Male Contacts

Female Contacts

Male EO (Electro-Oceanic) Connectors — Male EO connectors may be cleaned by rubbing the contacts with a cloth that has been covered with a light coat of metal polishing compound or other mild abrasives. Use enough pressure to remove the corrosion build-up. Always keep a thin coat of silicone grease on the connectors to preserve the rubber parts.

Female EO Connectors — Proper care of female EO Connectors should include rinsing them thoroughly with fresh water. Take a cotton swab and clean any excess grease that may have accumulated in the connector. If corrosion is suspected, clean the connector with a cotton swab and a dab of metal polishing compound. Then reapply silicone grease to the interior of the connector.

Nikonos Connector — Connectors for Nikonos cameras may be cleaned with a toothbrush. The contacts should be cleaned with a mild abrasive, such as the eraser end of a long typewriter eraser. Take care to remove any eraser particles that may accumulate as a result of the cleaning.

IKELITE CONNECTOR

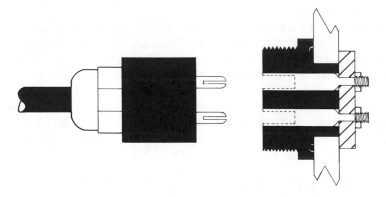

Ikelite Connectors — The male ends of Ikelite connectors may be cleaned with a toothbrush. The tiny space between the pins may be cleaned by drawing a piece of 600 grit wet/dry sandpaper through them slowly back and forth until all signs of corrosion are removed.

Female Ikelite Connectors — These connectors are difficult to clean. Try removing the cotton fibers from the end of a cotton swab. Dip the end in a metal polishing compound. Then insert it into the pin hole, using a swirling motion to clean out any corrosion. Take another swab with the cotton removed and repeat the procedure, this time to remove any excess polishing compound.

Rubber Pin Seal — The rubber pin seal for the Ikelite connector should also be kept clean. Remove it from the connector. Moisten a toothbrush in alcohol, then gently clean the entire seal with a light circular rubbing motion. After cleaning, wipe down with a light amount of silicone grease.

UNDERWATER LIGHT SOURCES

Underwater light sources presently range from the small instamatic type flash cubes to the sophisticated hi-voltage capacitor strobe units. While it is beyond the scope of this text to deal with every model individually, the most popularly used strobes and flash units require similar maintenance procedures.

Flash Bulbs — Flash bulbs have long been a friend of the underwater photographer, and they are still in wide use, even by the professionals. Because flash units are less expensive than strobes, many novices learn basic lighting techniques with flash bulbs, and continue to use them to supplement other photographic work.

BASIC FLASH CIRCUIT

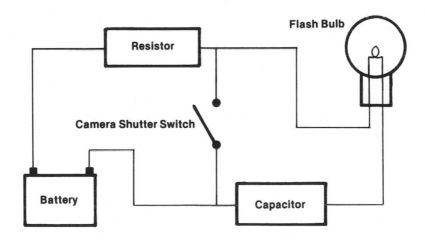

Most conventional flash units ignite the bulb with a battery capacitor power pack. The batter charges the capacitor. Then, as the shutter is activated in the camera, it discharges electrical energy stored in the capacitor to the flash bulb, thereby igniting the combustible filler inside the bulb.

Maintenance for Flash Units — The most common problem that may occur with flash units is the possibility of corrosion in the flash bulb socket. To prevent this, flush the sockets well with fresh water after every dive. If a light corrosion becomes apparent, try filling the socket with naval jelly or a similar mild rust remover. Let sit the recommended time, then flush with fresh water while moving the spring up and down. This should remove any corrosion that has begun to form in the socket.

If excessive corrosion is found in the flash socket, disassemble the flash socket assembly very carefully without removing any parts that you can not easily reassemble yourself. Clean off the corrosion that has formed on any of the disassembled parts with a rust remover, such as naval jelly. Then give the parts a light coat of WD-40 before reassembling.

Unused Bulbs — Unused flash bulbs that have been immersed in salt water should be rinsed in warm, fresh water. If their bases are allowed to corrode, they may provide a poor contact when used again. If excessive corrosion forms at the base of the bulb, sand the bottom electrical contact lightly to insure proper contact. Use a glove to protect your hand when removing spent bulbs. Some types of bulbs may crumble in your hand, causing cuts with the sharp glass particles.

Exposed Wires — Wires that are exposed in flash sockets are prone to breakage. The best type of socket is the type that does not use a wire in the socket to provide power to the bulb. Flash units using connector wires that are exposed to salt water must be continually inspected for corrosion, as the sea water may be forced under pressure in between the insulation and the exposed wire. Corrosion appears within the wires as a light, powdery substance. If this is detected, cut the wire back to remove the corroded length, and reinstall the wire exactly as it was before.

Strobes — Electronic light sources are highly sophisticated mechanisms which convert electrical energy to light. Whether using a housed or submersible strobe, do not try to do any internal repairs yourself on the strobe. Possible damage to the strobe or to yourself could result due to the dangers involved in working with high voltage and the possibility of severe electrical shock. Always follow the manufacturer's recommendations and instructions carefully.

Keep strobe O-rings and their seats clean and well-greased. Inspect the O-ring seats periodically for cleanliness and check for signs of scratches or cracks. Rinse the strobe free of salt water after using it. Before inspecting anything in the interior make sure that the capacitor has been discharged and the batteries have been removed. Do not use metal objects inside the strobe. Inspect the battery compartment for any signs of corrosion. Check all controls on the strobe or housing for stiffness and freedom of operation. Lubricate the controls when necessary.

Before storing strobes in between dives, the battery should be removed. If the strobe is the submersible type, the O-ring should also be removed to prolong its watertight effectiveness. If you store it in an envelope in the interior of the strobe, you won't forget to replace it when you use the strobe again.

BASIC STROBE CIRCUIT

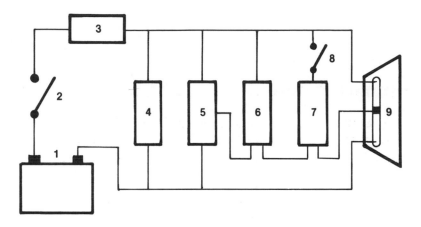

1. Battery 2. On/Off Switch 3. Resistor 4. Capacitor 5. Resistor 6. Capacitor 7. Pulse Unit 8. Camera Shutter Switch 9. Flash Tube.

Rechargeable Batteries — Most of the rechargeable batteries manufactured for commercial use in underwater strobe units are made of nickel-cadmium cells, and are thus called "ni-cad" batteries. The best way to maintain ni-cad batteries at their level of optimum efficiency is to follow the manufacturer's instructions carefully, particularly concerning how often the battery should be charged when in storage. Never recharge a battery beyond the manufacturer's specified time. Chargers with automatic shut-offs are best to use, but if your charger lacks this feature, be sure to watch the time carefully.

Do not let rechargeable batteries become completely discharged, as the polarity may be reversed when recharging again, resulting in possible damage to the cells. Always recharge the battery as soon as possible after you have depleted its cycle through use with your strobe. If you use rechargeable batteries that require long recharging periods, you might want to use two or more battery packs to alternate in your strobe, particularly while traveling. Also, when traveling, assure that the electrical source required to recharge your battery is the same as your charge, or take along a converter.

Disposable Batteries — Disposable batteries should be stored in the refrigerator to prolong their life. High voltage batteries should be handled very carefully, as rough handling (bumping or banging) may short one of the cells in the battery. The possibility of electrical shock is also present any time the battery is subjected to careless handling. Follow the manufacturer's warnings and instructions printed on the battery casing.

If any signs of bulging or leakage are detected on the exterior of the battery, it must be replaced. If you are photographing frequently with disposable batteries, whether low-voltage or hi-voltage, you can extend the life of the battery by using two batteries to alternate their use. Giving batteries a rest in between use can prolong their life.

FLOODED EQUIPMENT

The subject of what to do with flooded cameras and strobes is still a controversial one, and in many cases will depend upon the extent of the flooding. Most manufacturers recommend that the only action that should be taken is to place the damaged equipment in an airtight container and ship it to their nearest repair facilities immediately. Some independent camera repair facilities, however, do suggest that you give the flooded equipment a good fresh water rinse (depending upon the extent of the flooding) before sending it to them for disassembly and further repairs.

Many underwater photographers often find themselves with flooded equipment in remote places miles away from anywhere. As a result, they have developed their own techniques for field stripping and rinsing out cameras and strobes, which often includes the use of alcohol baths to facilitate evaporation of moisture inside the camera. While these procedures are generally not endorsed by manufacturers, since there is always a possibility of further damage to the camera, some have been field tested with a high degree of success.

If you find yourself with flooded camera equipment in a situation where repair facilities may be days or even weeks away, you will have to be the final judge of your best course of action. The following procedure may help lessen the amount of corrosion taking place inside the flooded equipment, and could possibly restore your camera to working condition again. However, this should be considered a ''last resort'' procedure for extensive flooding.

1. Open the housing, camera, or strobe and drain out all of the sea

water.   (Always turn strobes to the *off* position before opening the housing.) Remove all camera equipment from their housings.

2. Do not rewind the film in your camera if water is dripping out of the back of the camera, as this could force salt water further inside the mechanisms. Remove the film from the camera.

3. Remove power packs or batteries from strobes only after the strobe has been allowed to sit five to ten minutes in a dry place to insure that the capacitor is fully discharged.   Never attempt to disassemble or repair a flooded strobe yourself due to the high risk of electrical shock.

4. Open up the flooded equipment as much as possible, without tearing apart anything that you can not easily reassemble yourself. For example, remove the base plate, the lens, the viewfinder, and the battery from your camera.

5. Immerse all flooded equipment parts in fresh water, which may be luke warm, but never hot. While submerged, operate all of the mechanisms on both the camera and the housing. Do this several times, changing fresh water each time.

6. Give the parts a final quick rinse in a solution of water and Isopropyl alcohol to facilitate rapid drying. A weak solution should be used, such as one part alcohol to ten parts water, as the use of full strength alcohol could remove the adhesives and lubricants inside the camera and cause additional damage. If no alcohol is available, use just fresh water, and preferably distilled water.

7. Dry the equipment immediately, using the best method you can to insure rapid and complete drying. For example, use a hairdryer, a gentle stream of air from your scuba tank, or place the equipment in a warm environment such as the engine room of a boat or in a box lined with tinfoil with a 100-watt bulb inside. Activate all controls when drying, to eliminate any traces of water left inside.

8. After the equipment has been thoroughly dried, place it in an airtight container and try to get it to a qualified repairman as soon as you can.

Rinsing out a flooded camera or strobe is only a temporary step towards restoring it to its original condition. It is not a substitute for a competent camera repair facility. Even if the equipment seems to be functioning perfectly well after it has been rinsed with fresh water and alcohol, it should be checked over by a qualified repairman as soon afterwards as possible.

PHOTO MAINTENANCE KIT

Many of the parts and tools that you may include in your own photo maintenance kit will depend upon the unique features of your particular system, as well how often you use it and how frequently or how far you travel with it. Use the following list of suggested items as a basis upon

A sturdy plastic or metal container can be used to assemble a maintenance kit for your photographic equipment. Include a generous supply of spare O-rings, and include instruction and owner's manuals as well as your personal photographic log.

which to assemble a kit that will fit your photographic needs. And remember, the more secluded and remote the dive site, the more spare parts and tools you will want to include.

A Sturdy Container — Use a sturdy metal or a lightweight plastic container with a compartmentalized interior for assembling your kit. The container should seal tightly and have a secure latch.

Extra O-Rings — These are a must. Include a generous supply of them, making sure that you have at least one spare for every size O-ring in your camera system.

Lens Cleaning Fluid and Tissues — Manufactured by leading photographic companies, these should not be substituted by other inferior or abrasive types of tissue that could damage lenses.

Lint-Free Soft Cloth — Good for cleaning the camera body, or for just general cleaning purposes.

Paper Towels — Used for drying water from equipment.

Rubbing Alcohol — Good for general cleaning purposes, as well as possible use in rinsing a flooded camera or strobe.

Can of WD-40 — Useful in reducing corrosion around metal screws, threads, bolts on release snaps on housing and strobes.

Wet/Dry Sandpaper — 600 grit is good for cleaning male ends of connectors and contacts, but should be used cautiously.

Pencil-type Typewriter Eraser — Provides a mild abrasive to clean battery contacts and connector contacts in cameras.

Extra Batteries — Include those that fit your strobe and camera system.

Extra Screws and Nuts — For major fittings in camera or strobe housings.

Electrical Adaptor — For overseas travel, carry proper electrical adaptors and converters for rechargeable strobes.

Duct Tape or Electrical Tape — Miscellaneous uses . . . splicing, taping guide numbers on your equipment, repairs, etc.

Small Flashlight — For peering into hard-to-see recesses. Can also double as a modeling light on your strobe if it is the submersible type.

Owner's Manuals, Reference Charts, Log Books — Your camera maintenance kit is a good place to keep reference materials dry and accessible.

Metal Polishing Compound — for removing corrosion.

Silicone Grease — for lubrication of parts and O-rings.

Cotton Swabs — Excellent for a variety of cleaning jobs, as well as for applying silicone in tight recesses and grooves.

Assorted Tools — These will depend upon your particular camera and strobe assembly. Use the suggested list and tailor it to suit the needs of your system.

1. *Jeweler's Screwdrivers* — Most screws on camera equipment are small enough to warrant including these in your kit.

2. *Larger Screwdrivers* — to be determined by the size of the screws on your own equipment. Screws are easily damaged by using the wrong size screwdriver, large or small.

3. *Allen Wrenches* — Usually only the smaller ones are needed for some equipment applications, such as on housing knobs.

4. *Crescent Wrenches* — Choose a smaller sized one of good quality.

5. *Pliers* — Both blunt and needle-nosed may be included.

6. *Small Wire Cutters* — Useful for rewiring jobs.

7. *Small Soldering Iron* — for emergency wiring jobs.

Assorted Brushes — Brushes of various sizes should be included.

1. *Small Wire Brush* — Used for cleaning threads on screws and bolts.

2. *Toothbrush* — Useful for cleaning O-rings, grooves, and connectors.

3. *Blower Brush* — Good for removing dust from lens and shutter curtains.

4. *Small Artist's Paint Brush* — Cut the bristles short and use it for those small, hard-to-get places to remove dust and particles.

Always exercise caution when using tools on your camera equipment. Camera parts are delicate and fragile. They can be easily damaged and lenses will scratch easily. Carelessness or overexertion with tools can cause needless damage to your equipment. When in doubt about any part of your camera equipment consult a qualified repair facility.

For Traveling Divers

The popularity of sportdiving goes far beyond its status as a weekend sport. So much, in fact, that thousands of divers each year travel to such exotic places as the Red Sea, the Caribbean, the Indian Ocean or almost any other place that promises unique underwater exploration. At the same time, new resorts arc springing up everywhere, beckoning divers to spend precious vacation time and money at their particular diving establishment.

Most vacation diving normally involves a healthy expenditure of both time and money. Whether traveling from Arizona to Mexico, from California to the Caribbean, from Maine to Florida, or to an exotic dive resort thousands of miles away, you can not afford to overlook even the smallest detail that might spoil your diving, your photos, or your physical comfort. Prior planning and knowledge can save a lot of disappointment, trauma and ultimately, money.

INVESTIGATE YOUR DESTINATION

Whether you choose a diving vacation from the pages of a colorful brochure, from your travel agent, from a magazine display advertisement or by word of mouth, find out about the facilities, travel requirements, and other important details yourself before you embark on your journey. Transfers from the airport to your hotel may or may not be included in the package price, for example, and these costs in some places can amount to a substantial sum. Check for details in advance, before you find yourself short of funds with unanticipated costs.

Diving Facilities — Are there dive shops, equipment rentals, and working air compressors available? If it is a live-aboard dive boat or a resort in a remote region, do they have a back-up compressor for unforeseen emergencies? Once you arrive there, you're at the mercy of their facilities. Just because you are traveling to a well-known international diving resort, don't assume that it will have everything your local dive shop does. Many dive resorts are still a little spartan, so check around and see if you can talk to someone who's been there before. Inquire at your local dive shop. It's quite likely that they may know something about the resort or someone's who's bccn there.

Equipment Requirements — If you are taking your own scuba tanks to another state or country, make sure that the tank has a current VIP sticker on it. If it doesn't, you may have to pay for a visual inspection before you will be allowed to purchase an airfill. For convenience and security, get your tank visuals at your local dive shop before taking them with you on your vacation.

Are your tanks out of hydro? Check the last date of the hydrostatic inspection stamped on the neck of the tank. If the date stamped on the tank is over five years old, chances are very good that you will not be able to fill the tank anywhere.

Travel Documents — Don't overlook obtaining the proper visas or permits for international travel, or you could be held up on a minor technicality and even forfeit your vacation. Does the country to which you will be traveling require any types of vaccinations? Inquire through their embassies or consuls before you leave, particularly if you are traveling to a remote location. If you are going to rough it in primitive conditions, you may want to get a tetanus shot as a precautionary measure. To avoid discomfort during your vacation, get your immunizations well in advance of your travel dates.

Custom Regulations — For international travel, investigate the customs regulations of your intended destination. Find out what you are allowed to bring into the country, as well as what you are *not* allowed to take out. A native shop may be happy to sell you a turtle shell or a rare seashell, but you may discover that it will only be promptly confiscated from you at the airport on your way out. Save yourself some aggravation, and be informed beforehand.

Register valuable items, such as cameras and watches, by their make and serial numbers with U.S. Customs before you leave the country. This way, you won't be liable for paying duty on them when you return to the country, especially if the items appear to be newly purchased. Save receipts of overseas purchases in order to make the proper customs declarations when returning.

Fish and Game Regulations — When traveling to a diving site outside of your home state, find out about the fish and game laws currently prevailing in your intended destination. If you plan on taking game, find out what species are protected (if any), what the game limits are, what the requirements are for a fishing license, and all regulations pertaining to vessels launched in their waters.

For international travel, call the nearest embassy or consul and inquire about their sportfishing regulations. Very few countries allow foreign divers to spear fish and take commercial game species, so don't assume that you can do anything that the natives do. Remember, you are a guest in their country, and are expected to obey their laws.

Marine Reserves — Find out if you will be diving in an underwater marine reserve, and respect its regulations. Many reserves and underwater parks are not posted as such, so inquire beforehand with the proper authorities.

In many of the inland areas of our country, some states do not allow you to dive in certain lakes or rivers. This may be due to such hidden hazards as strong currents, intake pipes, pollution or other hazards. Make a preliminary investigation with the local dive shop when you get there, and find out where the locals do most of their diving.

Weather Conditions — Research the weather conditions of your potential destination before leaving, and try to arrange to travel during the most favorable season. Don't be angry with your travel agent for booking a trip to Australia for you in monsoon season or to Mexico in hurricane season. After all, you requested those dates. It is your responsibility to investigate the weather conditions and choose your own travel dates.

Check around and find out if other divers travel to the resort you have in mind. Inquire at your local dive shop. Any information you can find will enhance your trip. With research and prior knowledge, you can avoid spending a rainy week in a hotel room lamenting a ruined diving vacation.

WHAT EQUIPMENT SHOULD I TAKE?

For resort and vacation diving, your equipment needs will, of course, be dictated by the climate and water temperature of your intended destination. If you have done enough research before traveling, you should have a pretty good idea of what items to bring for both comfort and necessity.

Mask, Snorkel, Fins — Always take your own set of mask, snorkel and fins. If you don't already own a set, then purchase them before the trip. The price you might pay for renting them elsewhere will more than make up for the price of buying your own. Many places don't even rent such items, since most divers always bring their own. In warmer climates, you may spend a lot of time snorkeling, and will use your mask, snorkel and fins constantly.

Tanks, Backpacks, Weights — Unless you are traveling to your destination by car, these items are usually too heavy and cumbersome to bother carrying with you. Most places that cater to sportdivers have a good supply of these items to rent, and the rental price will be a small fee to pay for not having to carry these heavy pieces of equipment around with you.

Try to estimate the proper amount of weight that you might need for diving so you don't waste a dive or two trying to adjust to too much or too little weight. A good rule of thumb to begin with in estimating your weight needs is the "10% of your body weight" rule if you will be wearing a full wetsuit of 3/16" or thicker. Start with weights equal to ten percent of your body weight, and add more if you tend to float. If you won't be wearing a wetsuit at all, then you usually won't need any weights unless you want to weight yourself a little heavier for photography or stability. Also, remember that some countries figure weight in kilos, not pounds.

Regulator, Gauges, BC's — Although these items can usually be rented at most diving resorts and shops, it is always a good idea to take your own with you if you have room in your baggage. You are used to diving with your own equipment, and may feel more comfortable in strange waters. You also have a better idea of what kind of shape your own regulator is in than a rental one, and consequently may feel more confident.

Wetsuit — Find out what the air and water temperature of your intended destination is. Ask others who have been there concerning wetsuit needs, taking into consideration the seasons and time of the year. In some parts of Mexico, for example, you can comfortably dive without a wetsuit during the summer, but winter water temperatures necessitate the use of a wetsuit.

If the water is warm, you may not even need to bring a light surf suit with you. Usually, swimsuits, jeans or a tee-shirt will suffice. In hot and humid climates, just suiting up can be an ordeal, no matter how thin the wetsuit may be. Generally, clothing to cover your arms and legs is needed for protection from stings or abrasions from sharp coral, but not necessarily for warmth.

Extras — Handy extra items that should always be included in your personal diving kit when you travel might include: an extra mask strap, a fin strap or two, snorkel keeper, extra pair of gloves, and extra CO_2 cartridges for your vest. Take at least one of each. These are not only good back-up items for emergencies, but they also make good barter or "tipping" items for the local divers. In remote places, these small items can be more highly prized than money, since they are not readily available and may take months to order.

Dive Tables — Bring your own set of dive tables and know how to use them. Don't rely on others around you to calculate depths, time and repetitive dives for you. You may think everyone knows the dive tables, but don't count on it. When cold is not a limiting factor, you can easily dive all day without realizing that you are approaching the danger zone. Also, divers in different countries may use tables that you are not used to, so play it safe, and bring your own.

Diver Certification Card — Always carry your diver certification card with you. Even though some resorts don't bother checking groups of divers, some do, and you'll never know when you might need to show it.

Make extra copies of your certification card. Leave one copy at home, and carry the other with you in your camera or dive bag. If your wallet is lost or stolen, this copy may enable you to obtain airfills and will facilitate in replacing the card when you return home.

To Replace a Lost Card — Search for your certification card well in advance of your departure date, so you can allow time to replace it if it has become lost or stolen. The following certifying agencies have their own procedures for replacing your card.

NAUI Certification — Contact *NAUI Headquarters,* 4650 Arrow Hiway, Suite F-1, Montclair, CA 91763. You should supply the following information: date of certification, instructor's name and number, certification registration number, etc. A small fee will be required to replace your card.

PADI Certification — Contact the research department at *PADI Headquarters,* 1243 E. Warner Ave., Santa Ana, CA 92705. A photo and small fee along with information pertaining to your certification is required to obtain a new card.

NASDS Certification — NASDS Headquarters recommends that you contact first the dive shop or instructor from which the initial certification was obtained, and request them to assist you in obtaining a new card. If the dive shop is out of business or you cannot locate the instructor, write to NASDS Headquarters, P.O. Box 17067, Long Beach, CA 90807, and they will send you the proper forms to fill out.

YMCA Certification — In order to replace a lost YMCA certification, write to *YMCA Underwater Activities Center,* P.O. Box 1547, Key West, FL 33040. A small fee along with the following information will be required: your instructor's name, date and location of the dive class, and your social security number.

SSI Certification — To replace a lost SSI certification card, contact *Scuba Schools International,* 2619 Canton Court, Ft. Collins, Colorado 80525.

L.A. County Certification — Contact the L.A. County Parks and Recreation, Attn: Aquatics Division, 419-East 192nd Street, Carson, CA 90746.

C.M.A.S. Certification — Divers who travel frequently to international resorts may be interested in obtaining the French CMAS certification. Information may be obtained by writing to: CMAS International, 34 Rue Ducolisee, 75008 Paris, France. Or, if you are currently certified through NAUI, you can obtain a cross-certification through NAUI Headquarters by sending a request with your current address, a copy of your present NAUI certification, and a fee of $10.00.

Driver's License — In addition to your passport or visa, this is usually always accepted as additional proof of identification. It may also be necessary for renting jeeps or cars for island tours if the opportunity presents itself. For driving, some countries require that you obtain an international driver's license. Check with your local automobile club or the nearest embassy or consul to find out how to obtain one if needed.

Spearguns — Generally, resort diving does not include game taking. Most reefs are protected for sightseeing, and spearfishing is illegal. Therefore, don't go prepared to shoot big fish or load up on lobster and conch or abalone. Unless you will be "roughing it" on an island in some remote area where you may need to spear an occasional fish for dinner, it is best to leave your spearguns home. Some countries get nervous when you list "spear gun" on your equipment declaration list at their port of entry, and groups of divers have been delayed for hours simply because of the word "gun".

First-Aid Needs — Boat trips to reefs at dive resorts usually take less time than excursions off either of our own coastlines, so seasick pills are not a necessity unless you are easily upset by even short boat trips. If you will be aboard a boat for extended periods of time, you may want to include some type of seasick remedy in your first aid kit.

If you will be traveling to remote areas where facilities are primitive, or extremely limited, ask your family doctor to prescribe some type of mild antibiotic or other "preventative" medicine for combatting foreign bacteria. You may also want to have him issue a prescription for "Lomatil", or any other type of medicine for intestinal upsets.

For prolonged diving in warm waters, include in your first aid kit a solution of 50% alcohol/50% glycerin to alleviate infections in the outer ear and help keep the eardrum dry. Such solutions are also excellent for periodically flushing out your regulator if you are diving in warm waters where bacteria could flourish in the moist recesses of your regulator.

Aspirin, insect repellent, and a good sunscreen (preferably containing PABA) are also handy for traveling. Dive vacations are often cut short due to overexposure to the sun during the first or second day of the trip. Use a good sunscreen liberally, or wear a hooded vest or a wetsuit with a hood for snorkeling. Long underwear, jeans or a long-sleeved tee-shirt will also keep the sun off your body while you're swimming or diving.

WHAT ABOUT CONTAMINATED AIR?

Traveling divers in particular should be especially aware of recognizing the sources and signs of contaminated air. Although most cases of contaminated airfills can be readily detected by smell or taste alone, there are odorless and tasteless contaminants that can bypass the usual sense detectors of the body. Traveling divers, especially in remote locations with limited facilities, should be able to recognize conditions that may indicate the compressor is pumping bad air, as well as the physical signs that can indicate he has received a bad air fill.

SCUBA PROTECTION FILTER

An added insurance against contaminated air and the damages it may cause are the SCUBA PROTECTION FILTERS, developed by Professional Scuba Repair (North Hollywood, CA). These units are designed to prevent contaminants from entering your air system, and are an excellent safeguard if you are concerned about the quality of air entering your breathing system.

Examine the Compressor — If you arrive at a resort with limited facilities in a remote area, ask to examine the air compressor before you go diving. Not all compressors in remote areas should be suspected of pumping bad air, but the remoteness and difficulty of obtaining spare parts for needed upkeep may contribute to poor maintenance of the compressor system. Check out the physical condition of the compressor, noting exterior signs that may indicate a potential for pumping contaminated air.

1. *Location* — Where is the compressor located? It should be located in a cool, dry area with at least four to five feet of clear space surrounding it on all sides to insure adequate ventilation. Lack of proper ventilation can cause the compressor to overheat and will place a strain on the filter system, which can allow bad air to enter your tank.

For gasoline powered compressors, make sure that the air intake on the compressor is located sufficiently away from the exhaust system of the engine. Portable compressors of this type should be used outdoors, if possible, so exhaust fumes can't circulate in the room and back into the air intake. Keep an eye on wind conditions. Place the air intake upwind of the exhaust, and be alert for wind shifts that could cause exhaust fumes to blow into the air intake. If filled indoors, make sure the exhaust is funneled well out of the room, through a doorway or window.

2. *Exterior Conditions* — Examine the exterior physical condition of the compressor. Has it been well maintained and do the components appear to be clean and free of an accumulation of grease or dirt? Filthy conditions surrounding the compressor can contribute to compressor malfunctions resulting in bad airfills. If dust enters your regulator from a bad airfill, it will greatly reduce the regulator's efficiency.

3. *Test, if Necessary* — If you suspect that you have received a bad air-fill, or if the compressor is in a doubtful condition, test the air compressor with a clean, white handkerchief or a thin piece of white cloth. Place the

cloth over the filler yoke of the compressor system, and allow the compressor to run for at least 30 to 45 seconds. Then examine the cloth for any signs of dirt or discoloration. If residue appears on the cloth, the presence of undetectable contaminants should also be suspected.

Physical Warning Signs — The easiest way to detect contaminated air is by simply smelling or tasting the air in the tank. Before the dive, it is a good idea to crack the valve slightly and see if any unusual odors may be detected from the air in the tank. Attach the regulator and take a few deep breaths from it, to detect any unusual tastes. Always trust your senses, and do not continue to dive with your tank if you smell or taste anything unusual coming from the tank or regulator.

If the compressor is oil-lubricated, the oil vapor present in the compressor system must be separated out through a mechanical separator that separates the oil and water vapor from the air that is to be purified. If the oil and water vapor are not separated out efficiently, they could pass downstream and easily destroy the chemical purifiers, remaining in the air that is pumped into your tank. The taste and smell of oil is easily identifiable in a contaminated airfill.

A common problem in compressors derives from water contaminating the filter beds. Silica gel and activated alumina were once popularly used as an absorbing material to remove contaminants from the air, and may still be found in some types of compressors. The taste of activated alumina has been described as an extremely sour and vinegar-like taste. Today, most compressors use molecular sieves for the absorption process.

Carbon Monoxide Contamination — Carbon monoxide is an odorless and tasteless contaminant that is difficult to detect prior to the onset of physical symptoms. Carbon monoxide can enter the air intake of a compressor from the exhaust of a gasoline powered compressor, or through proximity to automobile exhaust fumes. Symptoms of carbon monoxide poisoning usually include a tightening of the forehead, a pounding headache around the temples and a bright red color around the fingernails and lips. The physical symptoms of this type of poisoning are compounded when breathed under pressure.

Carbon Contamination — A faulty filtration system in an air compressor can cause an accumulation of carbon contamination in the tank and regulator. Carbon particles in the form of activated charcoal will pass from the compressor system into the scuba tank, and can cause malfunctions in the tank valve and regulator if allowed to persist.

Carbon contamination will usually not show up immediately, and may only be visibly noticeable after a number of airfills from the faulty compressor. Black, dry particles on the sintered filter of the first stage of the regulator are usually a good sign of this type of compressor malfunction. Air compressors with cartridge type filters are not subject to this type of filtration malfunction.

TRAVELING BY AIR

Traveling thousands of miles by air to reach exotic and remote diving destinations is becoming more and more common among divers. Often, such travel involves having to make two or three airline connections or involves a series of lay-overs at different points along the way. Traveling divers who find themselves keeping constant vigil over cumbersome scuba equipment and expensive photo gear often wish they had taken up tennis instead. Make traveling with your equipment as simple as possible for yourself, and as safe as possible for your equipment.

Send Luggage Ahead — Travel agents can't always guarantee the capability or reliability of airlines, although they do their best to insure maximum convenience for travelers. If you have a series of layovers to contend with in your travel itinerary, you may want to ask your home airline to ship your luggage directly to your destination. That way your luggage will arrive ahead of you, and you can avoid the risk of having it lost or delayed during any of the transfers. This is particularly convenient if you have lots of equipment to worry about.

Luggage Mix-ups — It doesn't happen often, but if you travel enough during the course of your lifetime, then chances are you may arrive at your destination without your luggage on at least one of your trips. Don't let this eventuality spoil your vacation.

Get in the habit of taking a small suitcase of necessities with you as carry-on baggage in the passenger section. This could include a change of clothes, toiletries, a bathing suit, your film and camera, and of course, your mask, snorkel and fins. Prescription masks, in particular, should always be included in your carry-on baggage. That way, you may be able to enjoy a few days of water activities while you are waiting for your delayed luggage to arrive.

Weight Limitations — Although you should thoroughly investigate the luggage and weight limitations of all of the airlines that you will be using to reach your destination, in most cases airline companies will not charge you extra for your diving equipment. Simply check it through as sporting equipment (exactly as you would golf bags or skiis), and the extra weight will usually not be charged. Be sure to pack it in a good sturdy bag, and see that it is properly labeled so you can readily identify it.

What About Scuba Tanks? — If you plan on transporting your scuba tanks by air, most airlines will require that you empty them of all compressed air. This should be done very slowly with the tank immersed in shallow water, while you hold the valve and allow the air to escape slowly. *Never* crack the valve and let all of the air escape rapidly. Label the tank with your name and address, and if possible, place it in some type of cardboard container. To avoid damage to the valve, either remove it from the tank and carry it in your luggage or wrap some type of cushioned, protective material or cover around it.

In the event that you are asked to open the tank during a customs check, familiarize yourself with the proper procedure for removing the valve without damaging the tank or the valve.

Deep Diving and Altitude —Divers should exercise extreme caution when traveling in high altitude mountainous terrain as well as when flying in an aircraft after diving. The elimination of inert gas from the body tissues following an exposure to pressure from diving normally continues for a period of 24 hours or more. The *NOAA Diving Manual* states: "Before flying in an aircraft in which the cabin atmosphere will be less than 8,000 feet (usually the case for most flights), a diver who has completed any number of dives on air, and decompressed following the U.S. Navy Standard Air Decompression Tables, should wait at sea level breathing air for the computed surface interval that allows him to be classified as a Group D diver in the U.S. Navy Repetitive Diving Table." (See Section 6, Paragraph 6.4).

Desaturating to Group D, however, does *not* apply in cases involving flying after saturation diving. In regards to this, NOAA states: "Before flying after a saturation exposure decompression, a delay of 36 hours is recommended." (See Section 12, Paragraph 12.6.4) It is also a good idea, particularly with smaller or older aircraft, to check with the pilot to verify the maximum planned cabin altitude and to let him know that divers are aboard. He may want to question them himself to prevent any emergency situations. In all cases, exercise extreme caution, and remember that a reduction in atmospheric pressure such as that experienced in most airline flights may be sufficient to cause the inert gas dissolved in body tissues to reappear in the form of bubbles, causing possible decompression sickness.

Decompression Meters — If you travel by air with a decompression meter among your diving equipment, don't forget to pack it away in a pressure-proof container. Containers designed specifically for this purpose can be purchased for your decompression meter through your local dive shop. This is an absolute must for air travel, since the decreased pressure at altitude could damage or knock the meter out of calibration.

TRAVELING WITH UNDERWATER PHOTO EQUIPMENT

Nothing could be more disappointing to a diver who has traveled long distances to enjoy a photo-diving vacation than to arrive with dysfunctional equipment due to some small detail inadvertantly overlooked.

Investigate the Facilities — Before departing to an international dive resort, find out what kind of power sources are available for charging strobes and underwater lights, as well as for operating other personal

The best way to travel with photography equipment is by packing all components in a custom environmental protective case. Several layers of foam can be cut to fit the specifications of your own photographic system. Airtight cases with secure latches provide the best protection.

equipment as hair dryers and razors. If necessary, purchase an electrical adaptor at an electronics or a department store before you leave. Most countries use 220 Volt and adaptors must be used.

When traveling to extremely remote areas, consider the fact that there may not be any source of electricity available at all. If not, be prepared with a back-up light source for photography such as flash bulbs, or bring an alternate means of charging your equipment.

Custom Regulations — Check into the customs regulations of the country to which you are traveling to find out if there are restrictions on the amount of film or camera equipment that you can bring with you. Also, it is wise to register your photo equipment by serial numbers with U. S. Customs before you depart the country, particularly if the equipment is brand new. This will assure that you won't have to pay duty on the equipment when bringing it back into the country.

Label Your Equipment — Mark each piece of camera equipment, if possible, and record the serial numbers in a safe place. Also mark your camera bags so they are readily identifiable by you. In case of theft or a baggage mix-up, you will have an easier time identifying your equipment and presenting proof of ownership.

Take your Own Film — Purchase all of the film you think you might use before you depart. Pack it in foil bags to protect it against airport x-rays. Once you get to a vacation area, the price of film will reflect the lack of competition and you may end up paying substantially more for it. Take an ample amount, and store it in a cool place. Take a variety of speed films with you in preparation for all types of weather and water conditions.

Air Travel — When traveling by plane, try to carry as much of your photo gear as you can with you in the passenger section of the plane. This way you can be assured of the handling it receives, rather than trusting it to a baggage compartment agent. You will also not have to risk losing it in baggage mix-ups.

Remove the O-rings from housings and strobes before boarding the plane. Airplane cabins are pressurized, but not to sea level pressure. Most long distance commercial jets fly at an altitude of 30,00 feet plus. At 30,000 feet the airplane cabin may be pressurized to an altitude equivalent of 6,000 to 8,000 feet, therefore creating a reduced amount of atmospheric pressure working on the seals of your equipment. If the differential pressure were great enough, the seals could be damaged or even forced out of the housing by the outward thrust caused by the internal pressure on the O-ring seals.

Nikonos Users — Remove the lens from the camera body and leave it off for the entire trip. If you wish to use the camera for aerial shots from within the plane, simply remove the O-ring on the lens and reassemble the camera. Don't forget, however, to replace this O-ring when you take it underwater again.

Protect Your Equipment — Make use of compact carrying cases to transport photography equipment. Choose a case that is lightweight yet sturdy, with tight seals and a secure latch. Choose a case that will fit the specifications of airline travel. It should be small enough to fit under the passenger seat of the cabin. A case measuring 21'' x 13'' x 6½'' will fill this requirement. A ladies' cosmetic case or overnight hand baggage will also work nicely.

Protect Your Investment

Once you've invested in a set of diving gear designed to meet your special diving needs and to provide you with safe and comfortable diving, a consideration of prime importance will be how to protect that investment. Proper handling and maintenance procedures will keep your gear in good shape, but there are also ways to protect your equipment by storing it properly and by observing a few precautions that could prevent easy rip-offs at home or while you're traveling.

STORING YOUR DIVING GEAR

If you are planning on storing your diving gear for an extended period of time (six months or more), there is a proper way to store every item to insure maximum longevity of your equipment. Don't let your gear pile up in a dusty corner of the garage hoping that it will serve you as well this year as it did last year. It may serve you, yes, but it probably won't last as long if you haven't paid attention to storing it properly.

Diving equipment should be stored in a cool, dry place, away from the harmful effects of heat, smog and other contaminants. All equipment should be rinsed and dried thoroughly before storing. Never store wet gear in closed bags or containers. Store your diving gear in an area that has a constant temperature.

A garage is generally not a good place to store diving gear, since it can be ice cold in the winter and hot and stuffy in the summer, and is exposed to contaminants from car exhausts. For prolonged storage of a year or longer you may want to consider storing your gear in airtight plastic bags. After placing the gear in the bag, remove as much air as you can from the bag by squeezing or sucking it out, then seal the bag securely. This will keep dust, ozone and other harmful chemicals and pollutants in the air away from your gear. A moderately cool refrigerator is also an excellent place to store underwater lights, batteries, slings and other rubber products.

Mask, Snorkel, Fins — Remove straps from all buckles. Tension retained in the rubber could cause cracking of the rubber, particularly if the rubber has received frequent use. Rubber portions should be wiped down with a light coat of silicone or Armor All, taking care to avoid contact with the face plate on the dive mask. Remove any excess silicone from the equipment.

Wetsuits — The best way to store a wetsuit is to lay it out flat with something bulky inside to help it retain its original shape and prevent hard creases from forming. For example, stuff the legs and arms with wadded up newspaper or foam. Do not fold it snugly in a box or stuff it in a bag for prolonged storage. If you must fold it, fold it loosely and do not let heavy items squash it or make indentations in the rubber. If you prefer to hang your wetsuit for storage, use a wide wooden or plastic hanger to avoid creasing the shoulders. However, hanging a wetsuit for a prolonged period may stretch the rubber.

Clean all zippers on the suit, then lubricate them with a silicone spray or beeswax, working the zippers up and down. Do not use oil-based products on the wetsuit or zipper.

Rubber-surfaced wetsuits ("skin suits") should be coated with a light layer of talcum powder inside and out to prevent the surfaces from sticking together, causing the rubber to rot. Use plain, not perfumed talc, as the perfume base in some powders can damage the rubber.

Regulators — Regulators are best stored by letting them lie flat. Do not coil the hoses tightly or allow them to hang by the first stage. Don't let anything heavy rest on the second stage, as it can be easily dented or distorted. Always make sure the dust cap is in place.

The rubber hoses may be coated with a silicone spray, but *never* spray the entire regulator. Just rub the mouthpiece and hose with silicone. Do not allow silicone to enter the second stage, as this can cause the exhaust valve to malfunction and may cause contamination to collect within the second stage.

Some manufacturers supply a spacing device or a wedge with the regulator to be inserted in the second stage to depress the purge button, thus relieving pressure on the second stage valve seat while the regulator is in storage. If your regulator uses such a device, make sure that the regulator has been thoroughly cleaned and dried before inserting the spacer or wedge.

Buoyancy Compensators — It is best to let buoyancy compensators lie flat for storage, with the vest partially inflated to prevent the inner surfaces from sticking together. The rubber hoses may be wiped down with silicone to protect the rubber. Before storage, the buoyancy compensator should be rinsed inside and out with a commercial BC conditioner or other fungus retarding agent to prevent the growth of undesirable bacteria inside the BC. Always make sure it is thoroughly dry on the *inside* before putting it away for storage.

Tanks — The backpack assembly and the boot should be removed from the tank. If the boot is the self-draining type, this may not be necessary. *Always* store the tank with at least 200 to 300 pounds of air pressure in it. Never allow a full tank or an empty tank to sit for extended periods of time. The tank should be stored in an upright position in a cool place.

Spearguns — The exterior of spearguns may be wiped down with a light coat of oil to prevent corrosion. Slings may be coated with a light amount of silicone or Armoral to protect the rubber.

Lights — Remove all batteries in underwater lights for storage, and leave the lights open to relieve pressure on the O-ring seals.

Knives — Diving knives should never be stored in wet sheaths. Make sure both the knife and sheath are completely dry before storing. Knives may be wiped down with a light coat of oil to prevent corrosion.

Gauges — Gauges are precision instruments and should be treated accordingly. Depth gauges, compasses, pressure gauges and Decompression meters should be stored in protective bags or cases to prevent them from becoming dented, scratched or knocked out of calibration. Do not let heavy equipment rest on them.

PROTECT YOUR EQUIPMENT FROM THEFT

Diving equipment is not as interchangeable as other types of sporting equipment may be. It would be difficult for you to suit up with your buddy's equipment, and then expect to enjoy a safe and comfortable dive. Most divers have customized equipment that fits their particular diving needs and that conforms to the contours of their physical features. This is necessary for both safety and comfort.

Therefore, if any or all of your diving equipment is stolen or lost, you are not only faced with a monetary loss, but you are also faced with the hassle of having to purchase new equipment that may take some time getting use to. And, diving equipment, like everything else, is not getting any cheaper. By taking a few simple steps to protect your equipment, you can not only reduce the risk of equipment thefts and losses, but may also increase the chances of recovery in the event of a theft.

Mark Your Gear — Mark all of your diving gear with identifying marks or numbers in a place that is readily noticeable. If the first set of markings wears off over a period of time, don't neglect to *remark* your equipment. Before marking any rubber products, remove the manufacturer's coating of preservative. Use a small amount of acetone or laquer thinner on steel wool and rub the area to be painted until all the preservative is gone. This also prepares the rubber to adhere better to the paint. Use a good colored marking paint to position your initials or other markings in a noticeable place.

Wetsuits can be marked with paint for identification purposes, but markings on the exterior tend to wear off rapidly. For more permanent markings, try embroidering markings or initials in a conspicuous place with colored nylon or Dacron thread, or sew identifying patches in place.

The best type of wetsuit marking you can have is a personally customized wetsuit. If you order a custom suit, tailored to your specifications, take advantage of the opportunity to order a custom color combination or design that is unique and can be readily identified by you. A suit with unique markings is also much easier to recover in case of a theft.

Plastic or Metal Products can be identified by engraving marks on them. Engrave your full name, or your driver's license number or social security number, rather than just initials or symbols. You may use an exacto knife or other sharp instrument, taking care not to cut too deeply into the surface of the product. The best method of marking is with an electric engraver, which can be purchased inexpensively at hardware stores. If you want to engrave something fragile, such as a diving watch, it is best to take it to a jeweler, who has smaller instruments designed to do the job.

KEEP PERMANENT RECORDS

Photograph Your Equipment — Assemble all of your gear together after it has been marked, and take a picture of it. In case of theft, you have tangible proof, along with your other receipts, of exactly what you own in order to have it replaced or recovered. Or, if it gets lost in a baggage mix-up on an airline, you can file a claim with the photograph to facilitate recovery. It is also useful for law enforcement authorities to use in recovering stolen goods, should a robbery occur involving your diving equipment.

Record Your Equipment — Keep a permanent record of vital information concerning your diving equipment. This should include the serial numbers, the date and place of purchase, model numers, brand and additional identifying marks. Duplicate the record and carry it with you in your wallet, and store one copy away in a safe place. Should any dispute arise concerning equipment ownership, you can quickly refer to your records and prove that you are the rightful owner. Because diving equipment is both expensive and easy to sell, it is often a prime target for quick thefts.

Use the pages included at the end of this chapter to record your personal diving equipment. In the case of your tank and regulator, you might also want to include a record of servicing, including overhauls, visuals, and hydros. Also, note if the equipment is under warrantee or not. Make duplicate copies and keep in two separate places. This information is also valuable in the event that you decide to sell your equipment, since it will indicate how often the equipment has been serviced.

KEEP YOUR EYE ON YOUR GEAR

At the Dive Site — Get into the neat habit of diving "in and out of your bag". Never leave loose equipment lying all over the beach or all over a dive boat. This is a sure invitation to an easy theft, or even a simple "mix-up" which won't be discovered until it's too late. Before you leave the beach or the boat, double check your equipment to make sure that all of your gear is in your bag, and that you haven't mixed it up with someone else's. If your gear is conspicuously marked, this should be a simple matter.

Traveling — Label your diving gear with identifying tags that you can easily recognize, but avoid identifying specifically the contents with such labels as "Cameras: Handle Carefully" or "Diving Equipment". If possible, use a bag that can be locked. This won't prevent anyone from stealing the entire bag to pick the lock at a later date, but it can prevent someone from lifting a regulator or other valuable piece of equipment from your bag when you're not looking. This is how many thefts occur at busy airports, where it might be too conspicuous to steal the entire piece of baggage.

Do not leave diving gear in a conspicuous place in the back of your car when you leave the vehicle unattended. Store it well out of sight. This also goes for other valuables that might be left in your car while beach diving. Take your key with you underwater, rather than hiding it under a tire or in the bushes. Then you know where it is. Also, as popular as diver's bumper stickers have become, a red and white striped flag may be a signal to a thief that you are a diver and might possibly have diving equipment in your car. At the beach, it may indicate that you will be away from your vehicle for at least an hour to complete your dive.

In Case of Theft — Whether you reside in a house or an apartment, keep your equipment fully insured. Replacing stolen equipment can be a costly undertaking if you have no insurance. Theft protection insurance is available for apartment dwellers as well as homeowners. Inquire with your local insurance companies, if you are not already insured. Also, make sure your present insurance does cover sports equipment. If not, have your insurance man attach a rider for you.

If a theft does occur, notify the police immediately, and give them the serial numbers and photographs of your equipment. With good identifying marks, it is often a short time before stolen equipment is recovered. If you act quickly, armed with records, you may see your diving gear again. Divers often make themselves easy targets for theft, by spreading wet diving gear all over their back yards or apartment patios.

PROTECT YOUR DIVING FUN

Every diver should assemble his own personal *Diving Kit,* to be thrown in his gear bag and carried along on every dive for minor emergencies and unforeseen situations. Often, a great deal of time and effort is expended in planning an excursion to a new dive site. Don't run the risk of having a dive ruined simply because you overlooked some minor item that could have saved the day.

The following is a list of suggested items that every diver may want to carry with him in a small container for minor emergencies. Consider the list of items, and delete or expand according to your personal diving needs. Add items unique to your situation to make it your personal diving kit.

Sturdy Waterproof Container — Select some type of sturdy, but com-

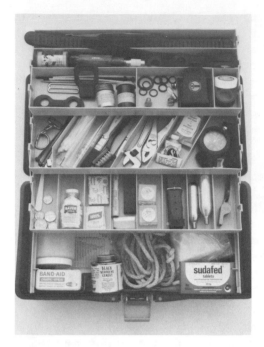

A maintenance kit, assembled in a sturdy compartmentalized container, will allow preparation for emergency equipment problems and field repairs. Diving gauges can also be stored in the kit, to prevent the rough handling they may receive in a gear bag.

pact, container with a secure seal (preferably watertight). If your needs are small, a sturdy zip-lock plastic bag may do the job. If you purchase a special container, make sure it is large enough to add additional items for vacation diving to other areas. You should also be able to lock the container for traveling purposes.

Extra Straps — Take one mask strap, one fin strap, and one snorkel keeper along with you. Even if you keep your equipment in top condition and are positive you'll never need an extra strap, you might make a friend for life if you have one to lend to a diving buddy in need.

Tank Valve O-Ring — This tiny O-ring has prevented many a diver from entering the water. Play it safe, and throw in two or three.

Special Regulator High Pressure Port Plug — A spare port plug with its O-ring can seal the port on the first stage of your regulator in case of a broken or leaking hose.

Silicone Lubricant — Include a stick or spray silicone to loosen stubborn zippers and lubricate O-rings.

Headache Remedy — Take some type of remedy for coping with aches from a strenuous dive or from noxious boat fumes.

Seasick Remedy — If you boat dive frequently, someone else may need this if you don't.

Leg Strap — An extra strap of any type can be used for a variety of purposes, such as attaching your goodie bag to your weight belt if you lose your snap or line.

First Aid Items — The contents of these will be determined by how far away from facilities you will be traveling, and whether or not there is a well-stocked first aid kit in your diving group or on the boat. Your personal first aid kit should include bandaids, sun burn lotions, decongestants and any prescription medication.

Loose Change — In case your wallet is stolen or lost while traveling, you can open your diving kit and find enough change for an emergency phone call.

In addition to the items that you might carry in a basic diving kit for minor emergencies, consider the following list of suggested items for traveling to a remote area or to a foreign country where facilities might be limited. For extended stays in remote areas, be liberal with the list and don't be afraid to overstock your kit. Since you are most likely spending quite a bit of time and money just to get to your diving destination, it makes sense to carry a well-stocked diving insurance kit along with you.

For Your Wetsuit:
1. Extra wetsuit material for patching.
2. Neoprene cement.
3. Spare zipper tab assembly.
4. Large needle and nylon or Dacron thread.
5. Wetsuit conditioner or baking soda.

For Your Buoyancy Compensator:
1. Spare oral inflator valve.
2. Extra CO^2 cartridges.
3. Vest Patching Kit.
4. Spare O-ring for interior of power inflator hose quick disconnect assembly.
5. BC conditioner.

For Your Regulator and Pressure Gauges
1. Spare exhaust valve.
2. Spare O-rings (for second stage hose, pressure gauge hoses, and inflator hose.)
3. Swivel assembly and small O-rings for your pressure gauge.
4. Spare O-ring for swivel assembly on regulator second stage valve.

Tank and Valve Assembly
1. Large O-rings for the valve to tank assembly.
2. Blow plug, disc and seal assembly to fit your tank.
3. Metric system adaptor from French to American regulator (if needed for foreign travel.)

Miscellaneous Needs
1. Extra buckle for weight belt or backpack.
2. Tools (jeweler's screwdriver set, phillips and standard screw drivers of various sizes, small pair of pliers, and a four to six-inch crescent wrench)
3. Can of WD-40 for corrosion prevention.
4. Duct tape or electricians tape.
5. Extra purge valves, if applicable to your equipment.
6. Lengths of nylon line and stainless steel wire.
7. Nylon tyraps.
8. Extra speartips, slings or sling material for spearguns.
9. Equipment instruction manuals and warrantees.
10. Personal equipment records and reference books.
11. Xerox copies of diving certification card.

Your Personal Equipment Record

MASK, SNORKEL, FINS

Date of Purchase _____

Place of Purchase _____

Brand _____

Model _____

Identifying Marks _____

_____

WETSUIT

Date of Purchase _____

Place of Purchase _____

Brand _____

Size _____

Identifying Marks _____

_____

BUOYANCY COMPENSATOR

Date of Purchase _____

Place of Purchase _____

Brand _____

Model _____

Identifying Marks _____

_____

PRESSURE GAUGE

Date of Purchase _____

Place of Purchase _____

Brand _____

Model _____

Identifying Marks _____

_____

DEPTH GAUGE

Date of Purchase _____

Place of Purchase _____

Brand _____

Model _____

Identifying Marks _____

_____

DECOMPRESSION METER

Date of Purchase _____

Place of Purchase _____

Brand _____

Serial Number _____

Other Marks _____

_____

COMPASS

Date of Purchase _____

Place of Purchase _____

Brand _____

Model _____

Identifying Marks _____

_____

OTHER: KNIFE, LIGHT, SPEARGUN

Date of Purchase _____

Place of Purchase _____

Brand _____

Model _____

Identifying Marks _____

_____

Equipment and Service Record

REGULATOR

Date of Purchase _____

Place of Purchase _____

Brand _____

Model _____

Serial Number _____

Overhauls _____

Other Servicing _____

_____

_____

REGULATOR (Octopus or additional)

Date of Purchase _____

Place of Purchase _____

Brand _____

Model _____

Serial Number _____

Overhauls _____

Other Servicing _____

_____

_____

TANK #1

Date of Purchase _____

Place of Purchase _____

Brand _____

Size _____

Serial Number _____

Valve Type _____

Visual Dates _____

Hydro Dates _____

Other Servicing _____

_____

_____

TANK #2

Date of Purchase _____

Place of Purchase _____

Brand _____

Size _____

Serial Number _____

Valve Type _____

Visual Dates _____

Hydro Dates _____

Other Servicing _____

_____

_____

ADDITIONAL TANKS

Date of Purchase _____

Place of Purchase _____

Brand _____

Size _____

Serial Number _____

Valve Types _____

Visual Dates _____

Hydro Dates _____

Other Servicing _____

_____

_____

ADDITIONAL EQUIPMENT

Type of Equipment _____

Date of Purchase _____

Place of Purchase _____

Brand _____

Size _____

Serial Number _____

Model _____

Service Record _____

_____

_____

INDEX

Bureau of explosives 37
Burst disc assembly 47-51
  and blow plugs 49, 50
  maintenance of 49, 50

C

Calibration, of gauges 91, 152
Cam pack 51, 53
Camera (see *Underwater Photography Equipment)*
Canadian Transportation Commission 38
Candle wax 19
Canvas strap pack 51
Capillary depth gauge 91, 92
  maintenance of 92
Carbon 9, 32, 68, 71, 150
  in compressor filters 150
  in silicone rubber 9
  in tanks 32
Carbon contamination 32, 150
Carbon dioxide (CO_2) cartridge 80, 81, 89, 146
  in buoyancy compensator 80, 81
  to install and remove 81
Carbon monoxide contamination 150
Carbon steel 114
Carbon-zinc batteries 120
Certification agencies, scuba 147
  to replace lost cards 147,
Chain vice 36, 43
  and removing tank valve 43
Chemical blown neoprene 17
Chlorine 9, 15, 65, 73
Closed bourdon tube gauge 93, 94
CMAS certification 147
CO_2 (see *Carbon Dioxide Cartridge)*
Compass, underwater 96, 97
Condemning, of scuba tank 37
Connectors 128, 133-135
  and corrosion 128, 133-135
Console, instrument 96, 112
Contaminated Air 148-150
Contamination, of diving equipment 32-35, 64-73, 84, 85, 88, 94, 148-150, 156
  in oral inflator 84, 85
  in power inflator 88

in pressure gauge 94
in regulator 65, 67-73, 156
in scuba tank 32, 35
in sintered filter 70-72
in tank valve 64
Contour pack 51
Control shaft 132, 133
Coral, hazards of 11, 17, 18, 23
Corrosion, of diving equipment 19, 29-35, 51, 53, 66, 69, 70-72, 95, 99, 108, 112, 118, 121, 123, 124 128-137, 142
  and burst disc 51
  and visual inspection 35
  effects of 30, 31
  in aluminum tanks 30, 31
  in back mounted weights 118
  in backpacks 53
  in batteries 121, 137
  in connector wires 136
  in connectors 128, 133-135
  in dive lights 123, 124
  in flash units 136, 142
  in hose fittings 66
  in knives 112
  in photography equipment 128-137
  in pressure gauges 95
  in regulators 69-72
  in spearguns 99, 108
  in steel tanks 29-32
  in zippers 19
  prevention of 32, 33, 35
Cotton swabs, uses of 129, 130, 135, 141
Cratering, in tanks 31
Crescent wrench 141, 162
Cross certification 147
Crossover assembly 47, 48
Customs regulations 144, 153

D

Dacron thread, uses of 18, 19, 22-26, 105-108, 157
  in knee pads 23
  in spearguns 105, 106, 108
  in spine pads 24
  in wetsuits 18, 26
  to repair zippers 19

168

Power surge 120
Prescription masks 151
Pressure reduction 55, 56, 58, 63
Pull rod, and J valve 42
Purchasing used tanks 37, 38
Purge button 64, 65, 72, 156
Purge valve 14, 162
  to install 14

Q

Quick disconnect hose fitting 86, 89
Quick disconnect pack 51, 53
Quick dump valve 78, 86
Quick release buckle 116, 118

R

Rechargeable batteries 120-122, 137,
  138
Reducer adaptor 44
Regulator assembly 55-74, 146, 156,
  161, 164
  accessories for 73, 74
  and travel 146
  disassembly of 69, 70
  first stage 58-61
  handling of 64
  maintenance of 65-68
  overhaul procedure 68-70
  record of 164
  second stage 62, 63
  servicing of 57
  storage of 64, 156
  troubleshooting of 70-73
  tune-up for 73
  types of 55
Repairs, to diving equipment
  12-14, 24-26, 78-80
  damaged buckles 13, 14
  faulty purge valves 14
  for masks and fins 12-14
  patching buoyancy compensators
  78-80
  replacing mask lenses 12
  to wetsuits 24-26
Repetitive dives 120, 146, 152
Reserve mechanism 40-43
  see also J Valve

Retaining pin, in buckles 13, 14
Retaining ring, in masks 16
Rubber — *see Neoprene Rubber*
Rubber pin seal, on Nikonos
  connector 135
Rubber tubing, for spearguns 104-108
Rust, in diving equipment 29-31,
  68, 112
  in dive knives 112
  in regulators 68
  in scuba tanks 29-31
  in steel tanks 30
  removal of 29-31

S

Safety mechanism, on spearguns
  102, 103, 109
Salt water, in diving equipment 30-32,
  68, 71, 73, 94, 124, 125,
  136, 138, 139
  in connector wires 136
  in photography equipment 138, 139
  in pressure gauges 94
  in regulator assembly 68, 71, 73
  in scuba tanks 30-32
  in underwater housings 124, 125
Sandblasting 32
Saturation diving 152
Schroeder valve 80
Screwdriver, uses of 82, 83, 141, 162
Scuba cylinder — *see Tanks*
Sealed bourdon tube gauge 93
Seams, 18, 19, 78, 79
Second stage assembly, 62, 63, 69,
  73, 74, 86, 156
  and silicone 156
  downstream valve 62, 63
  exhaust valve 63, 69
  octopus attachment 73, 74, 86
  pilot valve 63
Shaft, in spearguns 99, 100
Shock absorber 104, 105
  how to assemble 104, 105
Shot belt 115, 117
Silica gel 131
Silicone lubricant, uses of 15, 19, 28
  31, 46, 47, 67, 80, 90, 108, 112
  129, 130, 133-135, 156, 157, 160

Wetsuit cement — *see Neoprene
    Cement*
Wetsuit conditioner 28
Wishbone assembly, for slings 106-108
Wrenches 43-46, 66

X

X-rays, and film 153

Y

YMCA certification 147

Z

Zinc coating 29, 32
Zippers 19, 28, 156
    and storage 156
    for beach diving 19
    in drysuits 28
    in wetsuits 19
    maintenance of 19, 28